THE CİTY
BENEATH THE
SNOW

THE CITY BENEATH THE SNOW

stories

MARJORIE KOWALSKI COLE

UNIVERSITY OF ALASKA PRESS • FAIRBANKS

University of Alaska Press
P.O. Box 756240
Fairbanks, AK 99775-6240

ISBN 978-1-60223-183-2 (cloth); 978-1-60223-155-9 (paper); 978-1-60223-156-6 (electronic)

Library of Congress Cataloging-in-Publication Data
Cole, Marjorie Kowalski.
The city beneath the snow : stories / Marjorie Kowalski Cole.
     p. cm.
ISBN 978-1-60223-183-2 (cloth : acid-free paper) — 978-1-60223-155-9 (pbk. : acid-free paper) — ISBN 978-1-60223-156-6 (electronic book)
I. Title.
PS3603.O429C58 2012
813'.6—dc23
                          2011032941

Cover design by Wanda Chin.
Cover art: *Awaiting Relocation, 1st Avenue Cabin* by Tanya Clayton
Interior design by Dixon Jones, Elmer E. Rasmuson Library Graphics

Thanks to the editors of these journals, where the following stories first appeared:
Alaska Quarterly Review: "The Music of Desire"
Arkansas Review/Kansas Quarterly: "Grace"
Chattahoochee Review: "Holly, 1968"; "Star of the Sea"
Cirque: "Pieta"
Cream City Review: "Highways"; "The City Beneath the Snow"
Kalliope: "The Same Salt"
Passages North: "Psalm for Anabel"
Room of One's Own: "Aurora Borealis"
The Northern Review: "With This Body"

The poem "March Snow" by Wendell Berry is reprinted with permission of
            Counterpoint Press.

Printed in the United States

Other Books in the Alaska Literary Series

Peggy Shumaker, series editor

The Cormorant Hunter's Wife by Joan Kane (poetry)
The Rabbits Could Sing by Amber Thomas (poetry)

Praise for Marjorie Kowalski Cole

A Spell on the Water

"This novel held me rapt. I couldn't put it down, couldn't wait to finish—some stories should be like this—like life. I am so impressed with Cole's craft, her wisdom, the way she can hold whole worlds of relationship and conflict in the palm of her hand as a writer."
—Barbara Kingsolver

Correcting the Landscape

"...her writing is simple, vivid and gorgeous."

—*Eugene Register-Guard*

"...ushers in a remarkable new talent. Critics have lined up to praise this book."—*Tucson Citizen*

"Cole's style is subtle but engrossing.... The reader hardly notices that she is making a very strong statement about preserving the land and its people. It is quite a debut."—*Booklist*

"...written in a sure hand without being obtuse, poetic without being florid.... another sign that Alaska writers are beginning... to map out a much-needed place on the literary landscape."—*Anchorage Daily News* "an important book that will make a home inside everyone who reads it." —Salem *Statesman-Journal*

"...a book about strength—of the land and in our lives."—*The Oregonian*

"A body of prose conceived in the soul of a poet." —*The Missoulian*

"What gives the novel insight...is the portrayal of ordinary people trying to juggle loss, failure, love, and conscience every day, to find an "expectation that's better than hope"....Nobody's perfect in *Correcting the Landscape*. That's good, because neither are we." —*Orion*

"A powerful portrayal of a community imperiled by allegiances within and beyond itself, *Correcting the Landscape* is subtle, politically intelligent, and personally mesmerizing—everything I love in a good story."—Barbara Kingsolver

"What an engaging, important book this is! *Correcting the Landscape* is a superbly written novel with a keen conscience and a clear, true-voiced narrator...."—Naomi Shihab Nye

Inside, Outside, Morningside

". . . she shares her passion for the domestic and the sacred with equal measures of tenderness and frankness. We should all be grateful for her words."—Anne Coray

The morning lights

whiteness that has touched the world

perfectly as air.

In the whitened country

under the still fall of the snow

only the river, like a brown earth,

taking all falling darkly

into itself, moves.

—Wendell Berry, "March Snow"

CONTENTS

Highways

For his fifty-second birthday Eamon Castle gave himself an art class at the University of Alaska: figure drawing. That first night he walked past a horn quintet practicing in the Fine Arts Hall as he hunted for the art studio. The tootling of the horns made him feel ridiculous. It took a lot of bravado to start these things, and the horn music reminded him of just how much. But, he knew, the feeling would pass. You push forward.

The twelve art students, strangers to each other and to each other's talent, shuffled out of parkas and straddled benches. The instructor was leaning against a window ledge chatting lazily and looking around. Without any warning, in walked a twenty-year-old girl without a stitch on. Her bottom was firm; her back rose lean and well muscled to straight, lovely shoulders. Her skin had never seen a tanning parlor. She climbed a few steps up a ladder then turned around to face the class.

Eamon looked at the floor. He wanted to cough or pull the beard he'd recently shaved, but he noticed not a sound from the other students. The instructor, a beanpole of a guy at least Eamon's age, began to talk about the human skeleton. He gestured calmly toward the girl's hips. She had short blonde braids and intelligent blue eyes.

Eamon had a marriage of twenty-five years, a grown daughter of his own, the unsettled memory of one affair, and a framed nude by Kathe Kollewitz in his shop—his wife, Bonnie, wouldn't have it inside the house. As a highway engineer he had been in enough western towns and topless clubs to feel beyond the point of astonishment. But now his heart was beating a little fast and he was briefly without any references. What to do? I guess, he thought, eyeing the disinterested faces around him, I've been out of circulation. Twenty minutes later, having made his first sketches, he thought happily, no, it's not that. A beautiful woman ought to take you by surprise.

Eamon knew he had no real talent, but in his fifties he realized that inclination was enough—was itself a gift. His fingers longed to rise up from the boilerplate of environmental impact statements and take reverent note of the world around him. Still, walking around the room during breaks—the instructor urged them to look over each other's work—Eamon felt shy of his stiff, unpracticed lines. His charcoal inched around the page as though he were trying to connect the dots. The gap between his hand and eye announced a complete innocence of art. He rubbed his bare chin and tried to accept the rung on the ladder he'd be occupying for the next twelve weeks.

During the second class, a week later, he noticed that the woman next to him sometimes turned from the model to make a quick, emphatic sketch of one of the other students. She drew the model with great care, taking every minute allowed, so that her pictures looked as accurate and frail as tracings; but these other sketches were dashed off in bold lines. Eamon decided to try that. He looked around, then more closely at the woman next to him, and saw a large hole in the knee of her faded jeans. Her bare knee showed square and lean, just like the model's. She wore thick brown braids, too, from which much of her hair escaped. Her hands, one moving swiftly over the paper, one on her leg, were thin, strong-looking, with the skin pulled tightly over prominent tendons.

In the hall during a break, he noticed that she kept her eyes down, or directed to a far corner, as she smoked. Then she caught his gaze and smiled, in a relaxed and friendly way as if she were not so much reserved as simply thinking. She wore hiking boots and carried her cigarettes in the pocket of a long, shabby, man's sweater. She must have been in her early thirties.

The next week he said to her, as they pried out thumbtacks and slipped paper into folders, "Feels like the end of a long, long day."

"I know that feeling," she replied with a nod, but with something held back. She paused in wrapping a muffler around her neck. "What do you do?"

"I build roads," he began. He meant to disparage the activity, but he immediately realized he was doing the opposite. I'm Big Eamon Castle and I jes' build roads. "I run the highway department," he tried again. "I mean I'm an engineer."

She said she designed display ads at the local newspaper. "This," she said, waving a hand at the studio, "is the best part of the day." She picked up her folder. It was ten below tonight; blue long johns showed through the hole in her jeans. Her parka didn't look warm enough to Eamon, but her face gleamed inside a pink wool helmet. A trial or two had worn valleys below her eyes, but her eyes were a clear, vivid brown, direct and friendly. She walked down the hall with her folder under her arm and out into the night.

Eamon did not hanker for solitude himself, he got enough of that at home, and he included a stop at the local tavern into his weekly routine. He struck up a friendship with the instructor. They made a habit of it, and Eamon wondered if he could get the woman to join them sometime. As if by contrast to the smoky, cinderblock tavern where conversations floated across the room over the jukebox, she appeared in his mind quiet and intense, glowing. She had things on her mind, a destination. He liked that.

Her name was Frances, and he decided after a few weeks that hers were the most interesting drawings in the class. Other students were more proficient but locked into one style. Frances didn't always take the easy road. She would lean into the paper, her left hand on her leg and her right hand holding the charcoal just above its irrevocable first mark, and she'd stare at the model as if she were taking aim at a Dall sheep. Her back would go tense as a cable. After a successful drawing she'd smile at nothing and walk up and down the hall during break, life in her face, smoking. She smoked a supermarket brand of cigarettes. They bore the same label as the canned peaches and toilet paper Eamon's wife bought.

He brought Frances a cup of coffee one day from the student center.

"You smoke too much," he said, surprising himself. He realized instantly he was searching for some footing with her. She considered his remark and put her cigarettes away.

"All right, one less," she said, smiling. Eamon felt a sudden rush of joy at his small success. One more step and he'd be courting her.

In twenty-five years of marriage, he had actually strayed only once. During the unbelievably adrenalin-charged season they built the haul road to the oil fields at Prudhoe Bay, he somehow found time—as if the extra energy he was expending actually increased his supply—to pursue the affections of a lovely young woman who had joined the Teamsters Union to drive the crew bus. She was a graduate student in French and Russian; she talked a lot about terrible things in European history—Armenia, the Spanish Civil War, pogroms. She gave him the Kathe Kollewitz print. But her face, in the twenty-four-hour sunlight, had the unasked-for beauty of the landscape around them. She was fresh and fair, with a wide, slow smile and a complete innocence of marriage. It broke Eamon's heart when she left Alaska at the end of the summer. Oil money, he told himself, it was oil money that drove everyone wild. The money eroded all the usual connections, just as water erodes everything in its path.

After that he started taking night classes. He liked the varied combinations of people that each class title attracted. He liked to see all these people off duty, being themselves. He'd taken philosophy,

Alaskan literature, Alaska Native literature in translation, and senior men's water polo. And now he was learning to draw, learning to see. The hardest part was letting go and trusting himself to make the bold stroke. He admired the assurance in Frances's work and he admired it more because he could see that it frequently deserted her. She would spend ten minutes on the line between forearm, wrist, and hand.

One night in late February the temperature swung down to minus forty. When he saw Frances zipping up insulated pants over her jeans and beginning to wrap her face, Eamon stopped on his way out of the studio. He touched her shoulder.

"It's cold tonight. How far do you walk?"

"Three miles." She read his expression and added, "Uphill. It keeps me warm."

"I'll give you a ride."

"I'm used to it."

"It's too cold," he said. "Your sketchbook will snap."

She smiled. "Well, thank you, then."

Inside the warm cab of Eamon's truck, she pulled off her helmet and the loose ends of her hair followed it.

"What is it you're used to," Eamon asked, "walking or cold weather?"

"Both," she said, smiling.

She directed him to a cabin in the hills west of the university. He was pleased to see that she obviously lived alone. She said she had running water from a holding tank, electric lights, and a woodstove. Her landlord lived within sight in a fancy log chalet.

"Hard work, the simple life," he said.

"It's what you make time for, like anything else," she replied, looking at her home from the warm cab of the truck. He didn't turn the engine off. The heater purred around them; he imagined her cabin was stone cold. To his delight she began to talk. "I used to grind my own flour, things like that, thought nothing of it. I walk as much as possible so that I'll stay used to it. I knew a guy once who even walked out to the airport when he had to catch a plane. You just leave early, he said.

He wouldn't accept a ride. I'm not that far gone, though. Thank you for the lift."

"Sure," Eamon said. "Why did you stop? Grinding flour?"

"I live in town now. I buy flour at Safeway, like everyone else. Oh, this was out on Woodchopper Creek, a long time ago." She said *crick*, like someone from the bush.

"Did you draw then?" he persisted.

"This and that. Mostly objects. The lantern on the table, Easter eggs in a rusty cup, the view from the window. Onions. Those things are easy. Not like a human figure." She put her hand on the door handle and paused. "You are much improved," she said.

"I'm sorry?"

She laughed, shyly. "Your sketches show that you're really enjoying the class. Putting something into it."

"That's nice of you to say. At my age, taking up art."

"I mean it. Any age, it's the doing that makes all the difference. Getting out and doing it. And it's hard, I know. Not fruit in a bowl that only changes with the light, but live ones. You know she's going to get up and shake herself in two minutes or twenty, and never come back to that pose; you'll never see it again. Is that what makes each one so beautiful?"

"I don't know."

"I don't mean to philosophize."

Her deep-set eyes impressed him. Like two passengers on a bus, he thought, they were looking out at the same scenery, he and Frances.

"Goodnight," he said.

He would have liked to see her in, but considering that she usually walked this far alone, it seemed an awkward courtesy. He didn't insist.

The very next week, spring came in a rush, or at least the beginning of spring: clean, wet clouds sailed through the valley and the snow started to settle as it evaporated, growing dirtier and dirtier, pockmarked with a winter's trash. A glacial pond grew in front of the Fine Arts building. Arriving for class early, Eamon couldn't have predicted his delight in finding Frances sitting on the puddingstone bench in front of the building, smoking and staring at booted students splashing to class. Her loneliness attracted him, he realized. They walked to the studio together.

Eamon had traveled in most of road-accessible Alaska; he had done his part to make it road-accessible. But he had never been to Woodchopper Creek, though he knew something of it. It lay above the Yukon River in a hidden, tortured patch of wilderness: creeks, game trails, and one all-but-illegal blaze made by a miner with a Caterpillar tractor years ago were the only access. She hadn't lived there alone. No mistake. It took one of those wild throwbacks, those socially undeveloped but ambitious youngsters so often drawn to Alaska, to want to set up housekeeping in a place like that. Eamon had never been tempted in that direction. He could not imagine hunkering down in those hills, laying out a line of traps as if you owned the place—sabotaging the game trails under the stunted black spruce trees, while back at the cabin the slavey kneads dough of hand-ground wheat berries, splits stove wood, surprises her man with homemade Christmas ornaments. Then, waiting—there must have been lots of waiting—takes out her watercolors and begins to sketch what she sees from the table. Arranges a pile of onions on a chipped tin plate.

She wasn't for that world, Frances, not someone who got so high on a twenty-minute pose that she paced the hall with burning cheeks, smiling in spite of herself. You're jealous, Eamon told himself, of the boy who had her alone out there. Before those trenches got worn under her eyes, before she started smoking.

Then she agreed to come out for a beer. There were six of them; she said little but laughed readily at the jokes and dipped into the bowl of pretzel sticks Eamon slid toward her every time she reached for her cigarettes. Eamon drove her home. He wanted so badly to come into her cabin that he didn't trust himself to speak.

"I'll see you after spring break," she said.

A week with no class. He had forgotten.

"Ah," he said, disappointed.

"Eamon."

"Yes?"

"Are you married?" She rolled down the window but made no move to get out.

"Yes."

"Are you sorry I asked?"

"You must understand," he said at last. "There are things in a person's life.... No, there are things outside of it, things good in themselves, like your company..." Like a clearing in the trees, he thought. But he stopped; he didn't want to be talking them into something, using a line. "There are unexpected things, yet familiar, too. I'm all too familiar to myself, in fact. What the hell, talking this way, just talking like this—I know better. But I hereby disregard what I know."

She laughed. "Well then. I'm not saying I don't want to be with you. I'm just saying don't keep it from me. Okay?"

"Deal."

They looked at each other as she opened the door and let it swing open. She smiled. "Week after next," she said.

He reached out his arm and rested a hand on the back of her head, feeling the weight and shape of her skull, the thickness of her hair. He thought of his fingers going into that hair, how it would fill his hands. He thought of turning her head toward his. Instead he lifted a braid and tugged it gently. He put his hand on the shift.

"Good night," he said.

She walked slowly away, looking down as she picked her steps in the rough, wet snow. He watched the white V of her neck between her braids fade into the gray light.

In the driveway of his own home—four bedrooms, a family room, detached shop, cyclone-fenced dog run—he sat behind the wheel for a long time. He was going to come out of this bad. Women had changed. It was all new to him now, and he didn't look good to himself. There was still his marriage, which appeared to him like a matched five-foot shelf of books that no one ever opened. Frances, warm and alive and needy, wanted company. She wanted a human exchange. And he wanted it. Was that reason enough to turn his back on this thing, his marriage, this edifice that had so gradually accrued size and beauty and strangeness and hostility over the last twenty-five years?

He thought of quiet dark eyes signaling to him, an awkward grace of bent knees and powerful hands next to him, week after week in the studio.

Eamon slammed the truck door behind him. It's age you're running from. It's looking at this house, no different than a dozen others on this street, and wanting to start all over again with a girl and a cabin.

Only he wanted no such thing. No girl, no cabin. Frances was a woman, one marked by sad experiences. And she needed someone. Wholly, not him, with all the baggage of his life. Clear out. Bug out.

But no, he thought, that's crap. That's an ending point. And this is a beginning. I want to be with her. No, that's not quite it: I want to follow her. I want to follow her home. Oh, Jesus. It feels good to know that. It feels like spring is coming.

After Easter they had a male model, a tall young man whose hobbies were ballet and mountaineering. The muscles in his thigh were cliff-edged as a shoulder of granite. Eamon had trouble. In a week his fingers had gone stiff, and the boy's figure was so well-defined that the total impression eluded him.

And Frances: she had pinned her heavy brown hair into a bundle, and loose hairs waved around her face. She wore a red linen shirt with short sleeves but no collar. Her neck and arms were bare and freckled; her eyes were full of light, like clear coffee. Eamon struggled against his sketchbook for an hour. During break he stepped outside with the model, and the boy muttered with a short laugh that his girlfriend had taken this class one semester, and he'd forced himself during each pose not to look at her, not to think of her. Or he'd be sorry. That's the way, Eamon thought with admiration. Never mind the environment. Discipline your vision. Draw. During the second half of the class he reminded himself to concentrate.

Behind him the instructor stopped for a minute to study his work, then reached out with a long finger to make a suggestion. For one heady moment Eamon was no longer a hobbyist but a student. He had forced himself into the ranks.

After class he and Frances delayed leaving, as if by agreement. She held her parka lightly in her arms as if she didn't expect to need it. He touched her shoulder lightly.

"I'll drive you home," he said.

She nodded.

"It's becoming, your hair."

"Thank you."

At her cabin he came in without asking. She stoked the stove and made coffee, one cup at a time, with a plastic filter cone. There was a fifth of brandy on a scrubbed pine counter, and she splashed a generous amount into each cup. If she had seemed bold in the studio, she seemed shy again now. She put on the old, loose sweater over her red shirt, and when she moved magazines to one side of the small table and pulled out chairs, her fingers trembled. Her tablecloth bore a brilliant print of birds—cardinals, blue jays, and chickadees snacking on berries. He sat down with his cup and moved it from one bird to another, stood up again, and walked around. She bent over to peer into a broken piece of mirror propped on the kitchen counter and touched her hair.

Small as it was, the cabin seemed spacious to him because of the lack of furniture—and because nothing in it was his. A high bed was covered with a fading red quilt. A bookcase layered of boards and cinder blocks held as many jars and bowls of pencils and brushes as books. A heavy shortwave radio took up the top shelf. Above the bookcase were a few prints, tacked to the logs, and one framed pencil drawing of kohlrabi. He went closer to inspect it. They were meticulously rendered in fine crosshatch lines. He had rarely looked at any one object as closely as this drawing forced him to look at the bizarre roots and their forest of stems. They seemed more like sea vegetables than garden crops.

"You did this," he said, reading the signature.

"I definitely got kohlrabi out of my system with that one," she said. "But it turned out well." She had hardly moved from the kitchen corner. She felt in her pockets, and then turned to the drawer behind her, rummaging through it, dropping things on the counter. He went up behind her and took her by the shoulders. She seemed to move back against him. His heart pounded. He took the pins out of her hair, one by one, and it fell over his hands to her back. Then, holding her shoulders, he saw among the things she'd taken out of the drawer a colored snapshot with curled edges. He reached around her and picked it up. There was Frances at the top of a snowbank, grinning broadly down at the photographer, her face younger, fuller. Between her knees was a child, a wide laughing face inside a fur ruff, a big, bundled toddler gripping Frances's knees.

"Who is this?" he said softly.

"My daughter and me."

"Is this out on Woodchopper Creek?"

"Yeah."

Eamon sat down at the table. "How old is she?"

"She was three in that picture."

"And now?"

"I don't have children now. I had two, a girl and a boy. They were killed with their father in a plane crash."

Eamon held the picture on the table in front of him. She watched him steadily.

"When?"

"Six years ago."

In the picture, she wore a trapper's hat, with fur earflaps and a tongue of fur at her forehead. The red parka and the hat shouted I am of the bush! I am of the country! Now she sat across the table from him in her loose sweater, her hair rippling against her cheekbones, watching him. He reached across the space between them and stroked her sweater, as though she were a child whose clothes he were adjusting for school. His first instinct was to cover her, somehow. What a terrible secret to bear. His hands dropped back on the table. He had thought to please her with these hands, but she knew more of desire than he ever would. What's desire, but not having? Knowing full well the object you long for, in your heart and your memory and your blood, and not having?

"How do you survive a thing like that?" he asked, his throat full.

"Well, people have," she said at last. She turned back to the counter and finally located a pack of cigarettes. "After the—after it happened, after everything, I decided to take a cross-country trip. I did that for a lot of months. Driving. I crossed Canada and I came back through the Midwest. It surprised me how far you can go in this country on a tank of gas. It really isn't that big. Land ran out too soon for me."

She took a deep, relieved pull on a cigarette, sat down at the table, and looked at him. "Do you want to hear this?"

"Yes."

"In Michigan I went to art school for awhile, but there was no concentration. Once I could accomplish anything I wanted, move physical objects in space almost, just by concentrating. I could focus on things. Not anymore."

She leaned out an arm to use the sink as an ashtray.

"But if the wind was in my face, if the scenery was changing around me, I did all right. So I kept driving. And one morning, I stopped at this mountain pass in Washington State, at sunrise. I walked up a trail, away from the road, to this lookout. I was the only one there, except for squirrels and jays. It was gorgeous and astonishing. Red and glowing and full of sound: wind and birds and maybe the rocks creaking, I don't know. I had just crossed from the eastern side of the mountains to the western side and right at that moment I caught the smell of pine trees. It was real sharp, cut right through the cigarette smoke. And something happened."

She was silent for a moment. When she spoke again, her voice held a note of defiance mixed with awe, as if she didn't expect Eamon to completely believe her. As if she had told this story before and couldn't change a line of it.

"What happened was I woke up. The grief inside me had to move over for joy. For the first time it was displaced. I wasn't dead to myself anymore. I felt guilty to be there alone, but what could I do? It was my goddamned sunrise, mine alone."

"Yes," he said. She leaned toward him, her eyes alight.

"Because they were taken from me, I treasure the memory of that cabin, and the kids, and Russ; but I would not have stayed there the rest of my life. There were things I was tired of. We would have left. As it is, I didn't go through that stage of deciding to leave. I just lost it all. I lost everything, so I treasure every experience I had with them." She pulled air deep into her body. "I'll never be over it—you never are—but I remember my kids now, from time to time, with, you know, regular old amusement. I never thought that would happen to me again."

She dropped her cigarette into the sink and ran a quick splash of water. She sat back down and placed her hand on top of his.

"Never again flight," she said. "That is the worst thing. I've met people—well, never mind."

"What?"

"I mean to say, I'm better off than some. And I know it. Like right now."

He turned her hand over and pressed her wrist, as thought he could measure the courage that poured into her skilled fingers. Life rolled on, without asking our permission. The blood poured into her hands, the rocks creaked, the highways eroded under the weight of pilgrims, oil money sounded every time a truck roared over the Yukon River bridge. And everybody wanted it, to feel that life, to feel that energy. He wanted it, too.

He put her hand to his face and closed his eyes.

"Oh," she said. "Tell me I'm not in flight again."

He rose, reached for her, and pulled her up against himself. "Frances," he said, over and over, his heart rushing like some wild duck beating up out of the water. He kissed her.

She said, her mouth opening against his neck, "I knew it. I knew I would like this, I knew it." He rubbed her spine, down to her hip, as if he could imprint her body onto his. Never mind the road is crowded and cheap, never mind the crowds. Oh beautiful highway. He held her away from him and looked into her generous, eager face, and he thought, I will not let her go.

Holly, 1968

Holly Wiburg was five foot ten at seventeen, and strong. She gave her brother and his friends a boost over the junkyard fence. She hauled water in five-gallon jerry cans, and whenever she swung them up two at a time into her father's pickup, she was proud to strike another blow at all those soft, padded girls in school, weeping over boys or smoking in the can or practicing the splits for cheerleader tryouts. Never doing a man's work in their lives.

It pleased Holly to get ravenously hungry for her own moose stew on a fall evening. It pleased her to drop a blouse off her shoulders at night and see muscles, not bird bones, not fat.

She cried only twice in eight years: once when her mother died, and once the night the Lord called her name at the First Evangelical Church on Farmers Loop Road, and then she didn't cry again.

She looked forward to getting out of high school and into the university. The counselor, a pinched woman in a navy blue dress with a round white collar, said with gentleness as thick and false as rubber gloves, "You are probably not college material." Holly almost laughed in her face. She recognized bad advice when she heard it. She didn't even tell her dad what the woman said.

Sam Wiburg was a Christian, but he was also a secessionist. He believed Alaska should declare its independence from the United States. Above the junkyard he owned outside of Fairbanks flapped a giant, ragged Alaska flag, and the fence was plastered with his various bumper stickers. BLEEP, was one. "Bloodsucking Leeches in Public Office," said the fine print. BLEEP, BLEEP in red all over the junkyard fence didn't deter his customers. It was the only junkyard this side of town and everyone had junk to get rid of—or needed parts for some old truck or washing machine. Men made small talk; wandered between towers of hubcaps, range tops, rebar, and tires; estimated the worth of so many unidentifiable scraps of metal, all the while their ears out like sticky paper for another Sam Wiburg story to repeat back at the shop.

It wasn't easy being Sam Wiburg's daughter in Fairbanks. During the Golden Days Parade every summer, he used to march with the Sons of Norway. He wore a real Viking helmet with horns and swung a mace, and with his grin and his blue eyes and his seven-foot stride and his wolf skin chest protector, he made a colorful Son. Until the year he took a swing at the mayor with the mace, in full view of two hundred people, and was arrested for assault. He received a six-month sentence, suspended because he was a single parent.

Sam wrote letters to the editor—so many that the newspaper limited him to one per month. Radio talk shows filled the kitchen at night. He hammered at his targets—hippies, Communists, bureaucrats, fairies, Indians and Eskimos claiming rights to the land. Who owned Alaska? Who owned that oil they discovered on the North Slope of the Brooks Range? Alaskans did, Sam said, not the feds or tree-huggers or a few thousand Natives soft from the white man's handouts.

"I tell you, Holly, that man is a liar and a Red and not only that but an asshole," he told her, night after night, drying the supper dishes while the radio crackled and the same strident voices beat at the air.

Eventually he'd shout, "Oh, sweet Jesus," stick the towel in his belt, and lunge for the telephone. Holly would slip away to her bedroom at the back of the house. Sitting cross-legged on her bed she would take off her thick, round glasses and polish them with her shirttail, listening to his voice. It sounded at a distance like a pulley, a rusting steel pulley that someone was yanking desperately against the odds, with no help.

At the university things were different. There were people of all ages, some with less money than the Wiburgs. There were refugees from Eastern Europe, Pakistan, and Nepal. She thought of them as refugees anyway, thought of herself and her family as displaced too.

She met Duncan Jacobsen at a concert in the student center.

At first she tried to fit Duncan into the category of refugee. A reformed Hell's Angel, she called him. Not quite, he insisted, just a biker. But his bulky shoulders and the black hair over his collar and his twinkling eyes said to Holly, *outlaw*. Of course now he was a college student. He diligently hit the books in the all-night study room where she worked evenings, checking packsacks at the security desk and sternly fetching students' reserve copies of *Playboy*.

And she would be aware whenever he was in the room. Very aware. The seconds that ticked by seemed in themselves precious, like snow-flakes falling. Soon it would be time for her to go; they would drift toward the student center for cocoa. That would be her favorite time of day. Crossing the darkened plaza, slowly, with Duncan.

The night they met, at the folk music concert, Duncan sat at the edge of the stage playing a guitar, wearing black jeans and a black jacket. The mandolin player in the middle, Roy, was chairman of Campus Crusade for Christ. But this wasn't a religious gathering. It was just a session. Anyone could play.

Nonetheless Roy assumed leadership of the trio of musicians. Duncan Jacobsen on bass, he told the crowd, and Evie Jones on con-certina. Evie was a short, heavy girl with a wide smile, dressed in a long skirt and pac boots. Her hair, wild and loose, rippled around her face.

They played well together when they could agree on what to play. Roy kept suggesting a gospel tune—"Amazing Grace" or "My Father's House." Evie would swing one knee over the other so that her long johns flashed a slice of red above her boots, and say, "That one doesn't work so well on the concertina. Here's an old Irish love song. You guys know...?" And Roy would miss his chance again. It was such a subtle dispute that Holly thought no one else noticed it; then she saw Duncan's grin when it happened again. Holly smiled. She would have liked to hear "Amazing Grace"; there was no more beautiful song in the world, but she had to admire the girl's refusal to be told what to play.

So then all of a sudden Roy just swung right into it, before the girl could argue, and he quickly waved the audience into it, urging them to sing the refrain. Holly couldn't help but look right at Duncan.

Sure enough he grinned back at her.

She looked away and around the room, feeling too warm inside an old pink angora sweater she hadn't worn in years. Every September when she dug out her winter clothes, they seemed fewer and more threadbare. She must have worn this sweater since she was four-teen. It was a point of pride with her not to buy new clothes, but she wouldn't wear this sweater again. It itched, and when she put on her wool jacket, she nearly gave off sparks.

"Shall I be wafted to the skies," Roy sang. The audience softly, lovingly crooned the refrain and gave itself a round of applause. The musicians beamed at each other. Duncan stood up to fetch his guitar case, and Holly saw that he wasn't nearly as ruffian-looking standing up. His black beard and black hair were clean and trimmed. Even his Frisko jeans were clean.

She picked a circuitous route between the tables and chairs. Holly was not without experience, even if the experience was mostly slapping away the clumsy hand, walking fast, saying no, I'm not interested.

She hated the way boys' eyes made her feel, following her. Now she found that even that unpleasant experience was useful to her. It gave her something—a posture, an edge. A right to walk close by someone, just out of curiosity.

"How'd we do?" he said, as soon as she got close.

"Really nice," she said.

Easy. And after a while, they were friends. "I have a friend," she said to herself, walking home. She tried it out. "My friend. My real good friend, Duncan. There's this friend of mine." Now she had the featherbed around her, and something a little different under her skin.

She had thought once during a lonely time that all her friends were going to be Christians, but she never got around to asking Duncan his beliefs. She did let him know where she stood.

"I wasn't always a Christian," she told him, "but I am now, and it's a good thing to be."

He smiled and nodded. In return he told her about himself. He made a little money with a bluegrass group at a tavern south of town. He planned to find work this summer with the Department of Transportation, or maybe fighting forest fires. It's late in life to be in school, he said, but he had met lots of students near his age, even older.

"This is a different place," he said. "Not as tense as California. It's hard to live here, but people seem to have a good time with less, just the same."

"No one's got any money," said Holly.

"What about you?"

"I haven't got a nickel. But I wouldn't be anywhere else, even if I did. I can't leave home right now." She opened her lunch and found she had no appetite. Duncan did that to her. She offered him her lunch. He said no, but after a few minutes unwrapped a hard corn muffin from last night's dinner and took a bite.

"Have you traveled much?"

"Once to Seattle, when my mother died. That's it."

He considered this.

"What's it like, staying in one place?"

She wound her hair around her finger. What a question.

"Shall I guess?" he said.

She smiled, not at him but at the things he said. "Do that," she said.

"I have this theory. When you stay in one place, you accrue information about that place down at the microscopic level. When you're on the move, you're carrying your own place around with you. Like I'm from Amherst, Mass. Did I tell you that? I don't intend this to happen, but everywhere I go, it's Amherst meets L.A., Amherst meets Boise, Amherst meets the Badlands. Amherst rides an elephant in Thailand. It's a damn good feeling, don't get me wrong. When you settle down, though, you get to take off Amherst. Now, I'm saying you could tell me things about living here that would blow my mind, if you could pull them out of the pile of things you see as natural and everyday. What's in this muffin?"

"Cranberries."

"That's what I mean."

"I picked them."

"That's exactly what I mean." His words had a different quality; they were quiet, sorry. Authentic. She thought, I have something. Something with him.

Then she thought of her father's ramshackle, sprawling house and urethane-sprayed Quonset hut, the chicken yard, the vast junkyard on the highway where she and the boys wandered and hid and waited for the workday to end. No. That loneliness and clutter, being immersed in making a living, that wasn't an education. That couldn't be what Duncan wanted to say.

He finished the muffin and inspected the remaining contents of the bag—hard-boiled eggs, two short homegrown carrots, and a baggie of peanut brittle. Sam Wiburg had a terrific weakness for candy. The ideal food, he said. He bought it by the bucketful.

"What did you think of Seattle?"

"Oh, I was a child. Nine years old. It was in December and my aunt took me shopping downtown. There was a big model train going round in the window of a department store, and shining fake snow piled up around it, and the mannequins had snow on their shoulders. I wanted to touch it. I wanted to put my hand in the fake snow. My aunt bought me a new coat and a beret to go with it. A velvet beret." She shook her head, amazed that she once owned such a thing. What happened to it? "That's the first and last time in my life I've bought something new at a department store. So much luxury at your fingertips." She took a piece of the peanut brittle. "My dad felt real uncomfortable in cities, all of his life. He has to be surrounded by a world of his own making. I can't believe I'm saying this."

"Why not?"

"It sounds—harsh."

"Do you get along with your father?"

"Of course I do! What kind of a question is that?"

"It's an effort for some people, Holly. It's a decision. It doesn't always come easily."

"Well thank the Lord it does to me."

They sat in silence for a minute. He looked gentle, but very distant. She didn't mean to push aside his ideas; she meant something else. She had something important to tell him. What got in the way? It was like she was wearing her pink angora sweater again. Too old, too tight, the wrong impression. She wanted out of it, she wanted to tell Duncan the truth, but she didn't know what the truth would be. The truth was she loved her father. What was wrong with that? She wanted to be loyal. Loyal.

"I guess it isn't always easy," she said. "Maybe there is some effort to it."

He nodded. As if he understood. How could he understand? What did he know of her family, of anything? Was he short an education too? He wore a deep green chamois shirt that thickened his shoulders and arms. His dark brown eyes matched his hair.

21

"Would you like to come to dinner sometime?" she said. "I'm a good cook. We don't live on peanut brittle."

He laughed; she had said the wrong thing. Then he stopped laughing and looked oddly touched.

"Yes, I would, yes," he said. "Absolutely without a doubt."

"What's so funny?"

"Nothing. That was a nervous laugh. I would like to meet your family. Let's not put it off."

"You have a funny way of accepting an invitation." But she felt comfortable again.

"Well Holly," he said. "You have a funny way about you, too." She frowned.

"I like it," he said. He leaned forward and took the cuff of her sweater between his fingers. "There's a certain self-possession that's nice," he said, finally.

Dear Jesus, she thought. She didn't say anything.

That's how they came to be walking together down Sam Wiburg's twisting driveway a few days later. The bulldozed, rutted trail had been scoured by the cold into a tortured course around fat birch trees he couldn't bear to cut down. Her mother used to tap them, making birch syrup for pancakes. Holly remembered its disturbing taste intensely. It was sharp and wild, not like Lumberjack out of a bottle from the store. It was always a disappointment, like slightly burned blueberry cobbler.

Now the air itself smelled—of damp leaves and mushrooms and the stinking highbush cranberries that nobody liked, all around them, and then as they approached the house, of roofing tar. Rudy, her brother, was shooting baskets at a hoop nailed over the door of the Quonset hut.

"Holly's home!" he shouted over at the roof of the house.

Sam Wiburg came over the ridgeline. The house was a sprawling one-story mass of dark-stained plywood, two additions attached roughly to a central cabin. With a sudden desperate rush of anxiety, Holly noted the clutter all around, the red pickup blazing with its bumper stickers, the hammock of gray canvas between two trees near the house.

"Daddy, what are you doing up on the roof?" she shouted.

"Is that any way to greet your father?" A leather tool holster, lopsided with a heavy drill, pulled at his shirt and jeans. His face was dark with exertion but he smiled and waved. A good mood. He disappeared from sight and then reappeared at the side of the house, walking toward them, wiping a hand on his shirtfront.

Sam stood a few inches over six feet. Tight, dark red curls clung around the bald spot on top of his head and framed his massive square forehead where blue veins stood out when he was angry. Patches of skin on his cheekbones that turned bright red, like sunburn, whenever he was in the grip of an argument, were faded to pink. His brown plaid work shirt was ragged—breast pockets loose at the corners, buttons gone. He towered over Holly and Duncan, smiling, and held out a long arm with the loose sleeve dangling from his wrist.

"Well who is this?" he said.

"This is Duncan Jacobsen—he's staying to dinner."

"Welcome, welcome."

"What's wrong with the roof?" Holly persisted.

Sam peered at her and did not answer right away. Then he turned from shaking Duncan's hand and waved at a pile of aluminum sheets near the hammock.

"That goddamned newspaper is good for something after all. They are dumping these aluminum press plates for twenty cents apiece. When I was down there today the editor said, drive your pickup to the back door and I'll help you load up."

"Flashing," said Duncan.

"Flashing," said Sam. "Right around the stovepipe maybe. It's an experiment. I can't sell them till I can figure out a few uses."

"Can I help you?" said Duncan. *Oh, God,* thought Holly.

"I wouldn't mind the company."

Honor thy father and mother, thought Holly. I will bake a cake.

She went into the low, dark living room and began grabbing at toys, books, and clothes scattered on the chairs and sofa. There was a war inside her heart. Duncan wasn't part of this; this was her cross to bear, not his. He wouldn't understand. He would laugh. Worse, he would like her father—he would say the one, unforgivable thing: "Your father is a character, Holly." How she detested that. No one knew him. She didn't even know Sam Wiburg, but she hurt for him, and she took care of him.

She went into the kitchen and slammed the main ingredients for supper onto the counter—a butcher-paper package of mooseburger, a box of spaghetti, the canister of flour. Overhead, erratic sounds alarmed her. Footsteps creaked and the drill started and stopped. She looked around the kitchen trying to see it as if for the first time, as if through Duncan's eyes. It was a vast kitchen, like the bridge of a ship, Sam said. That was what her mother had wanted. A big kitchen full of windows, with a big table for the family.

But Sam did not run a tight ship. He never threw anything away, and stowed clutter came out from the walls about three feet all the way around every room, so the space they lived in was much smaller than the house appeared to be from outside. Counters and cabinets and chairs were made from recycled materials, odd scraps, milk boxes, and cable spools. It was a dark house, not positioned to catch the winter sun, in spite of the windows. Today there seemed to be vast distances between everything she needed—the stove, the refrigerator, the cabinets seemed miles apart, with crates of bottles, potatoes, rolled newspapers spoiling every corner.

She heard a painful metallic scraping from the roof.

She sifted the flour and then got down on her knees and bowed her head. "I want some humility," she said softly. "I want to be back in place with You." She crouched on the floor for several minutes, growing calmer. Rudy's basketball hitting the door of the Quonset hut calmed her; she could even hear the voices of the men on the roof.

Looking back later, Holly saw everything in slow motion, and she marveled at everyone's instinctive reactions. But at the time it was a crush of terrible things happening all at once. Still on her knees in a pool of silence, she heard a shout from Duncan, and at the same time a low, strange moan, like air whooshing from a tire. She was up and out the back door in a second. Rudy had the ball clutched to his chest and was staring at the roof of the house.

"What! What!" she shouted.

"Holly!" Duncan was shouting.

"Is he cut? Did he cut himself?" Holly saw the jagged, sawn edges of those plates in her mind, Sam minus an arm. Send Rudy for clean towels.

"No, no, he's sick or something. Get by the ladder." Holding Sam against him, Duncan inched down the roof, his heels digging into the shingles. Sam's fist came down upon his own chest, and he groaned.

"Hold the ladder, Rudy," Holly said. "Hold it fast." And she was up it, bracing her legs against the roof, pressing her waist into the eave, reaching for Sam. He slid against her.

"It hurts," he said, his voice like wood splitting.

"I got you, Daddy."

Contorting himself, Duncan tried to keep hold of Sam's shirt, but Holly took her father's full weight against her. Her legs shuddered. She took one step down, then another. He was taking painful, short gasps of air.

"I got you, Daddy," she repeated. "It's all right." But her balance nearly left her. She didn't move; only absolute stillness would save them. Her body became a brick wall. They would not fall. She waited, for a long time, as control came back into her muscles, and then she knew it was safe again. She was able to lean into the house. Her legs started shaking, almost like wild animals, but she was in charge. She started down, holding her father. She felt Rudy's arms behind her and ground under her feet. She sank to her knees and Sam crumbled with her. Her legs still shook, but she didn't need them anymore. She laid Sam's head on the ground and he stared at her with eyes the pale blue of ice. He looked astonished. Color was returning to his lips; they had turned blue.

"Your heart?" she whispered.

She could see the answer in his face.

Rudy and Duncan called an ambulance and brought out blankets. Holly didn't take her eyes from Sam's. His body was granite hard, and heavy, but the skin on his face was a fragile transparent cover to his agony. Fragile as the wing of a dragonfly.

"He's going to be okay," Duncan was saying next to her. "He's going to be okay."

"Holly's strong," said Rudy.

The ambulance drivers gave him oxygen, wrapped him in blankets, lifted him into the back of the ambulance. Holly, with her arm around Rudy, found this the most shocking thing of all—that they were taking Sam away, that the doors were closing.

"Can I ride with him?" she asked, confused. What should she do?

"Don't leave, Holly," said Rudy, pressing against her.

"I'll drive you to the hospital," Duncan was saying. He already had the keys to Sam's pickup. They climbed in and the truck roared to life. They followed the ambulance, the truck leaping over the ruts in the driveway, their three bodies hitting each other as the truck swayed from one side to another. She wrapped her brother in her arms. Her legs hurt but inside she felt strong and somehow ready for whatever was to come.

"You saved his life," said Duncan. "I couldn't hold him. You have some arms, Holly."

She looked at Duncan. Is that what happened?

"What, Holly?" said Rudy. Was she muttering?

She smiled at him and said clearly, "Those men in there know exactly what to do for Daddy. I promise you."

Rudy was big for a ten-year-old, like she had been. He had already lost a parent. She thought for a minute that he could lose another, today. No.

She should be praying, but she couldn't think of a line of prayer. She must pray—and yet, it didn't matter. She didn't want to think about praying right now; she wanted to absorb all of this. Holding Rudy, rocking down the road with her brother and her friend, a new sensation had fallen over her, like a new coat. Her skin seemed to inhale the space around her. She set Jesus off to one side, to think about later. They were approaching the intersection. Holly pressed herself back against the seat as Duncan leaned over the steering wheel to eyeball the highway. "Go on through," she cried, and he sailed past the stop sign.

The Music of Desire

NAOMI

We were at a junk shop in Seattle's University District, one of those places where room runs into room until all sounds of traffic fade and you're lost among surplus bar glasses and gunmetal green desks, rows of oak rockers and ugly, lumpy mattresses. Surplus items fill big slabs of space, but genuine junk is tucked in the crannies: weird bookends, martini shakers, old books, baby furniture, Depression-era ashtrays. This shop was managed by two tall, dark-haired guys in their late twenties—too young to be as sleazy, as focused on getting the highest prices for the shoddiest goods, as they appeared to be. It was not a young man's business. Maybe they'd inherited it. It was dim in there, just dim enough to make the customer suspend judgment. To start the critical mind daydreaming.

A clothesline crossed one aisle between the counters and towers, with a sign hung on it, "Office." Behind the clothesline in an island of breathing room, one of the young guys sat with his heels up on an opened drawer of a gunmetal desk and wrote in a notebook propped on his knee. That's where Johnny took the bookends, to ask in a completely uninterested tone, "How much for these?"

I was in graduate school then, and Johnny was visiting me on his annual buying trip from Fairbanks. Johnny was a collector. Not of any one thing, so much as furniture and furnishings for that one, great, ideal room in his imagination, that combination playroom-den-flying bridge that seemed to him the ideal setting for personal relaxation and robust, civilized intercourse. Social intercourse—good talk and funny stories, loud laughter, disrespect for time, that sort of thing. For this island of civilization he had dreamed up, Johnny spent all winter buying books and maps and lamps and what he called *dungshies*, the Chinese word for "things," he claimed—useless, decorative things. He lived with them awhile and then sold most of them at an annual garage sale in his backyard in Fairbanks. Johnny's garage sales were famous.

Some things he didn't sell. I could tell by the light in his face he wouldn't part with these bookends. They were ceramic scholars: each bookend was a little Middle Eastern guy perched on a ladder set against a bookcase. He was reading, and there were books piled around the ladder and filling the bookcase. The scholar wore glasses and had a beard, and he hunched over his book in complete engagement, unaware of everything beyond his eyes and the page. You could tell by his posture he was enjoying himself. Keenly. The whole thing was gaily painted in a variety of colors, though chipped in places. The scholar himself wore black trousers and a long gray coat. On the open page of his book were some letters, but I couldn't tell if they were Hebrew or Arabic.

I found them first, touched Johnny's waist, and said, "Look at these." He turned to me, and it was like the sun came out and showed a lot of things you couldn't see before. The sun came out in his face. His eyes lit up like a rushing river. "Oh," he said, "these are great!"

It's something to see someone you care for suddenly delighted—so pleased and surprised at the same time. He picked one up and we admired it, and then he hugged me of all things and said, "This is just what I've been looking for!"

He heard this music in his head. He just looked at those silly bookends and the music started. That's what it is, when you know you stand a good chance of getting what you want.

That's the kind of desire I like best. When you can choose to step into the music and out of it, at will, like a real artist. It wasn't going to break Johnny's heart if the sleazy guys claimed these were antiques and asked him for some outlandish, stupid price that would sour them forever if he bought them. But he did want them. It wouldn't break his heart, but it would demonstrate the injustice of the world. Because he heard that music, the kind you hear only when you stand a chance.

Johnny's face is pretty anyway, but it needs that light to be really something. He carried one back to the office island and said, "I was lookin' for some bookends. How much for these?" And then started touching and peering at stuff along the aisle there, hardly paying attention to the sleazy guy.

"I don't know. We haven't had these long. We like to keep everthin' thirty days, make sure it wasn't stolen."

"Oh, well, forget it then, I just need some bookends. You have any others? These are kinda funny, but it's just that I need something."

"Well, say, the two of them—five dollars."

Johnny took the bookends back without a word, without any sign of interest. Bored. He meandered back up the aisle. The cash register was at the front of the store. He wasn't going to cut a caper till we got out of there.

And then, boy, he did. It was almost like 1980 when the Phils won the Series and Johnny, who doesn't smoke, had to light up a cigar. When a guy feels flush, what can he do? Of course, after that day, though he admired them daily and enjoyed them, that light wasn't there—they were only ceramic bookends, after all. They'd hold up a row of books in that room. That room of his, that in his mind's eye, kept out the cold and the dark with good talk and good times. I know the room had some reclining chairs, a fat, polished Buddha the size of a large dog, baseballs from stadiums around the country. I don't know what else—it wasn't my room.

We set the bookends to work temporarily in my living room, and I told him, "I'd be this happy if I was going back home with you. I miss September in Fairbanks."

"That's the trouble with you, Naomi. Never happy right where you are."

"All right, all right, I'd be this happy if I was anywhere but facing another semester of school."

"That's why a lot of people quit. But don't you quit, Naomi."

There wasn't anybody else in the world who could say to me, "don't you quit," in just the right way. So I stayed and put in the time, and Johnny went off on his winter travels after mailing the bookends and a bunch of other stuff, including three boxes of used books, back to himself in Fairbanks. He worked seasonally, like a lot of Alaskans, giving himself a long vacation in the dead of winter. Since he was self-employed, he really did give himself the time off. Johnny's life was full of this wonderful decision-making power of his, islands of leisure. He had freed himself from "the factory."

For twelve years, Johnny edited his family's newspaper in upstate New York, a slave, he said, to the two o'clock roar of the press drums grinding to full power. One afternoon he was popping his first beer when a friend came by and said, "Bob Marshall climbed every peak in the Adirondacks over four thousand feet before he was twenty-five. What do you think it's like up there?"

"And that was it," Johnny says, in his economical way. They went to find out what it was like up there. One peak led to another, and a succession of them led him to Alaska. Of course it wasn't that tidy. It was a few more years before he shucked off the newspaper and realized that the freedom of the hills was a call that couldn't be met just by scaling a mountain after work. And in fact what he needed had little to do with mountaineering. In coming to Alaska, in punching out a rhythm to suit himself, he came home.

Raised in Fairbanks, I didn't know any of this until I left. But on the crowded rain-wet streets of Seattle, I had the sensation of turning into a weird mutant of myself, hunched and dripping and waiting. Like a polar bear at the zoo, padding round and round her concrete trough, never complaining, never fully alive.

Never happy right where you are? How much of that is up to us, anyway? Once my fingers got cold waiting for the bus. Only once, in three years, did I suffer red painful finger-ends that refused to warm up and turned dead white before I got home. I had lived in a place where you could be savaged by the cold any winter day. Destroyed by it, brought back to life by it. Wouldn't a person miss that?

What especially irked me was that Seattle was the same, day after day, for weeks at a time. Except for the explosion of azaleas in May, the seasons dragged. Each season had its own horse latitudes. Maybe it's stupid to live in a place like Fairbanks where fall is only a week long, but it sure is a beautiful week.

The one thing to Seattle's credit made my homesickness even worse: the views, so lovely and so plentiful, set people to daydreaming. With so many bodies of water below so many hills, you could catch a dozen celebrated views just in the course of going about your day. Seattle is full of fervent daydreamers: environmental spiritualists, druids, New Age mythologists, sexual pioneers, gourmet scavenger-cooks who go to great lengths to serve regional delicacies, like hunter-gatherers of antiquity—oh, a gamut of wounded, delicate, fun people. None of them very happy, but most of them in this intriguing state of flux. No one was quite the same, one week to the next.

Johnny in my living room was a challenge to these folks. A challenge to me. He was big, and he was happy. He did not cultivate subtle perceptions of his own feelings, and he did not mourn. He liked to tell stories of Alaskan characters, relate the news, but his anecdotes were far less appetizing, to most of us, than Johnny himself. He lay down on the rug after dinner and put his feet up on the couch and after a while he fell asleep like that, easy as a baby. I saw the unrelieved gold of the birch trees in his hair. I saw the cold, steady wind of autumn sweeping down the river valleys in the thin, roughened skin over his cheekbones. Or else, I made it all up, because I hungered for the place he had come from. Seattle encouraged fantasies. Mine were of home.

He came through Seattle to visit me, and, unchanged and full of life, he left again. In his indifference I knew what I missed most about Alaska: its indifference. Like a river roaring down from a glacier, swift and abrading, waves full of silt breaking over the rocks. If you are absolutely silent you can hear grains of silt sweeping over a boulder. Like a brush sweeping over a cymbal, you can hear it, despite the noise around you.

That's where I wanted to be, tucked into that indifference. Refreshed, at any price, by the cold air and the endless river.

Spark

Dear Sam, well I did it again Sam, I fuckin' did it again. Time rolls on, cried she. It's getting spring in Fairbanks, wet, warm, filthy, the snow pockmarked with the refuse of winter. Time for Johnny Costello's annual garage sale. I spent the winter in a Quonset hut out of town with a fellow who's been planning to build a house on that spot for the past ten years. God he worked on me like a magnet, I had no idea I was even being pulled in. I thought this one was going to last, Sam. I overlooked the obvious signs.

So I did it again, lost my heart and soul and a year of my life—to what?

As you can see, I'm not cheerful. But you asked what Johnny had for sale. Books and more books. This is your year. I suggest you come on up. Oh, Sam, I envy your gift for finding such joy in stuff. In books and books, all those things you collect. I don't see how you do it.

My paintings will be on sale too. Despite the weird living situation, it was a productive year in that regard. There was nothing else to do. And it was pretty out there on his acre of uncut birch woods. The Quonset had windows with printed cotton sheets hung up for curtains. And a woodstove and a little clothesline for his teabags. He used teabags three times.

Also, he smelled good. What can I say? He smelled like 1973. When I was eighteen, I'd go from the studio that always smelled like clay and turpentine over to the Student Center for a hamburger and macaroni salad, and some guy would get in line next to me in a Woolrich shirt giving off the smell of wood smoke and whammo. I was gone. But I guess you always knew your little sister was not the most disciplined artist.

So all right, Johnny's got books, maps, the usual records, no Persian Gulf souvenirs but a few pieces of the Berlin Wall, a gold rocker, and a bear spear. Can you make it? I wish I could offer you a place, but I'm moving in with a friend. It's not going to be a clean break.

I guess you know some people change with the times, move with times, and I just haven't figured out how to do that. Like choosing this guy as a boyfriend. It's so repetitive of me. Get this. He has the world's finest foundation. He finished it two years ago. He's obsessed with the foundation of this house he hasn't built. There's a good reason to care about foundations, but when's he going to get around to putting books on the walls? Like you, Sam. I'll tell you when. Never. God. I tell you, he touched my heart. I am so touched by these guys.

I'd like to put books on the walls someday. But most of the time that doesn't matter all that much to me. A girl in my situation ought to be thinking about kids I guess, but I'd rather think about yours. How are they? How's Annie?

Teaching went well this year. Doesn't take too much time. It's a kick having eighteen-year-olds again. They're sweet. I know we weren't sweet, but they are. Mighty ignorant of their own power, in spite of all the drugs and sex they do. In spite of how sophisticated they seem to be. You got to have a brick wall inside you to really paint. Christ, Sam, I forgot what inspired this letter! I got a One Percent for Art! That shows you how success-oriented I am. A high school on the Kenai Peninsula is adding a swimming pool, and I get ten thousand dollars for wall murals in the foyer. Not bad, right? Are you proud of me? Are you coming back for a visit? If not for Johnny's sale, then sometime soon I hope.

Brother, I'm proud of me, and I'm proud of you too. I hope I'm over this guy faster than last time. Maybe by the time the snow melts and it dries out around here. And you don't hear the tinkle tinkle of melting snow anymore. I'll plan on that. I just have to not see him. I guess what really clinched it for me, I mean to move in with him, was his dog. He was sweet to his dog. People give themselves away. I mean like the jig was up, when I saw him with his dog. Clover was her name. He named her after the jar of honey on his table when he got her, because she was honey-colored. Clover Honey.

I love you Sam. Hugs and kisses, Spark

JOHNNY

GIANT SINGLE MAN YARD SALE
EVERYTHING FROM A TO Z

Rain or Shine; Coffee and Cookies; Don't Be Left Out

Gas up the family auto, grab the permanent fund checks, and come have a look. Antiques, discards, mismatched and partial sets of things, memorabilia, Alaskana, Americana, games; original sofa-size paintings by well-fed artists; what is left of an entire jazz collection I once owned; musical instruments; treasures; and yes, useful items. Five mountain bikes. No Alcan, No Baja, No Dalton, No Dempster. And most especially folks this year:

BOOKS

My entire library is for sale. Travel books, great literature, Boy Scout Handbook circa 1953, philosophy, romance. This is the serious part. Good prices, a vast collection. The Library Must Go.

I WILL READ NO MORE FOREVER

Sam

Sam Ostness and his wife, Annie Lomen, talked about Spark's letter after dinner, while he washed and dried the dishes and she sat on the dining room floor, all spread with newspapers, making potato paintings with their four-year-old. Sam felt bad for Spark, in pain and so far away. He hated to know she was so lonely. For Annie, there was something in Spark's voice that she wanted to admire and praise. She couldn't pity her—she admired that vitality too much.

Spark was always in a bad way with men. Even when things were going good. But she still lived her own life, she still made a living, incredibly in Alaska, as an abstract painter. For as long as Annie had been part of the family, Spark's paintings had been absolutely unrecognizable. They weren't even abstract forms of recognizable things. And Spark would rather die than contemplate an Alaskan motif. She did not paint dogs, or mountains, or even rusty junk. It was amazing that a committee gave her a commission. They must have been so divided on the other applicants, they couldn't think straight.

"I wish she would stop torturing herself," Sam said.

Annie just shook her head. It was hard to explain the way she admired Spark. "I just love her letters," she said at last.

Sam looked at his wife, slowly carving a face in a potato and filling it with poster paint, saying not a word about what she was doing but letting the toddler discover the entire operation at her own pace—like the tiny explorer she was. Having married late, Sam was frequently amazed at the sweetness of married life.

What he didn't know was that Annie's head was full of silences. By sixteen, she had lost her father, two brothers, a sister-in-law, and two uncles to violent or accidental death, every death alcohol-driven. The rage and shame that colored her growing up meant, finally, silence. Too many voices were stilled, for one reason or another. And that's why she loved Spark. Spark was often miserable, but she was not dying, and she sure was not silent.

Annie liked her name, too. Spark. Sam and Spark had come up from Texas. They knew how to name people in Texas. It was such a pretty name, so full of their own mother's gratitude at having a healthy girl baby. Annie wanted to name her baby something like that. They chose Rita Merry. Rita Merry Ostness.

"If you go to Fairbanks," she said, "and I know you want to, take Spark a big bundle of pictures. It's so much fun, Sam, to show off the children! I hope God forgives me and doesn't think He has to bust my bubble."

"Of course not honey. It's no bubble."

Sam took off his rubber gloves and debated briefly joining his wife and child on the floor, but he decided to go into his office.

Sam's office, the biggest room in the house, was defined by bookcases on standards and brackets. Every wall was filled with books, and the room was filled with filing cabinets and three tables made from solid core doors, each covered with file boxes, papers, and more books. Retired from teaching, Sam was now a publisher. His little scholarly journal, released twice a year, contained bibliographic essays and transcripts of previously unknown or little-known manuscripts, all bearing on the history of Alaska. Sometimes a densely footnoted essay appeared by a respected scholar. Sam mailed six hundred copies of the journal to libraries and authors all over the world. Their subscriptions not only kept it in business but kept him supplied with delightful contacts. He had a scholarly friend in every capital north of fifty-three degrees. He received long, eccentric letters every week, and he responded diligently.

The office in his and Annie's Anchorage split-level was intended to be a recreation room, and for Sam, it not only came close, it crossed the line into play and intoxication. These diaries of missionaries and Bureau of Education teachers pursuing their desperate vocations in Alaska worked on him like a chemical enchantment. He knew perfectly well he was as insane as Don Quixote buried in books of chivalry, but Sam didn't care. He was truly happy. There was no happier man in Anchorage. That was his secret. And if sometimes between projects he looked around his office and noticed that he had to find his way between towers of cardboard in order to find his desk, and that the pictures of Annie and the children stuck into the frame of his bulletin board were lost under other notes, most of the time he felt only the pull of his deep fascination with the material. It drew him in. The written words of early Alaskans, their actual words, filled Sam with amazement.

Annie remained totally unaffected by the spell of history. She did not read his journal, though they kept a complete set in the living room. When he wanted to go to a conference in Helsinki or a library in Montreal or a used bookstore in Edmonton, she would say, after a moment's thought, the same thing: "Well, I think you should do that." She nodded thoughtfully at all his new purchases and said, "Yes, I'm glad you found this."

She was, perhaps, a little eccentric herself.

Where he would put the books he might find at Johnny's garage sale didn't concern either Sam or his wife. They would find a place. He wasn't likely to be interested in most of Johnny's books. Johnny fancied himself a cosmopolitan, a man of the world. He had to dip into everything. He had a lot of stuff that would be uninteresting to a true collector. Sam was going to Fairbanks only because there might be, there just might be the rare unexpected item, some precious document that he could not pass up.

And you never knew how many more sales there would be. Each one, as the years passed, was a comfort just for the repetition.

NAOMI

It rained. All-day rain is not exhilarating. When the end of my nose gets cold and drippy in the rain, I think about how far it is away from the rest of my face, and I wonder if I should get it bobbed. Instead of clear thinking, I'm contemplating a nose job. In the rain.

At Johnny's house, a big blue awning protected most of the goodies. Pieces of cut-apart clear Visqueen covered other things. The huge backyard was full of shapes.

Paintings to blow the mind were on display in his living room. In the past few years he had collected some artist friends. These were choice. The artists were struggling with—I mean wrestling against—their inherited ideas of the beautiful. Ideas they had been schooled on, ideas that worked on other landscapes, they found themselves using unconsciously on Alaska. It made them sick. They'd gag at their own work, then start wrestling against it, and out of the wrestling was born the savagery of these paintings. I guess this was what I was looking for. I stayed inside a long time, drinking a cup of coffee and cupping my long nose in my hand to make it warm.

I wondered if he had cleared out his bookcases to make room for these paintings. All except two low shelves that met in a corner, behind an easy chair. On the waist-high shelf, the scholar-bookends hunched endlessly, merrily, at work.

Spark Ostness brought her brother, Sam, inside to see her red-brown-rose-orange abstraction of the Tanana Valley. Spark was a generous, sloppy woman, dressed in a bright Guatemalan shirt-jacket, black jeans with a hole in one knee, and black break-up boots. She had vivid, staring blue eyes and wild red-blonde hair, and she waved her arms a lot as she spoke.

Sam was a narrow little man in a green work shirt. He had a nice, lean back.

"Look at the company I'm in," Spark said, waving at another painting by an artist whose prints appeared in every card shop in Alaska.

"Look at these bookends," said Sam. He picked one up. "Christ, where did Johnny find these?" He held one close and studied the scholar's book. "Hebrew," he said. His finger polished the tiny page.

Every fantasy I had spun (without meaning to) about this afternoon had me outside. A cool, pure wind would keep surprising us, would maybe direct Johnny and me around the corner of the house, and he would look down on me, and—something would happen. We would acknowledge and act on desire. Our impulses would move swiftly forward to revelation and joy. I would get to the east by sailing west. The smell of muddy spring in Fairbanks would excite us both. Johnny would pause, in his life he would pause—like a river stopping—and look at me.

Fantasies are for little minds and little people. I came inside with my cold nose and cup of coffee when I saw Johnny put his arm around some woman I had never met and say something, quiet and in code, to her hair. Now the rain fell, with no regard for lovers, or flowers, or rain barrels. It crushed last fall's brown and rotten leaves. It glittered on Spark's red hair and the toes of her boots.

You can't always reach that stillness at the center of the music. Sometimes you only hear the music in passing, a siren song. Even so, the astounding potential of that moment is not something you want to be alone with. You do not want to be alone with it.

"I like this one, too," Sam said, standing in front of a bright depiction of a river cutting through a rocky slope.

"I like it fine," Spark said, "but it's a comic book. It's alive, it works—but it's a comic book picture, Sam."

"What do you mean?"

"All right. It's musical, it's pretty. But look. There's the river, there's the rock, there's the frame: everything in its place. The river spills down like someone turned on a faucet. It's a fountain in a park, Sam, not a river in the hills."

"I don't see that."

"Ah, well."

"Naomi," Sam turned to me. "What about this picture? What do you think?"

"I was sitting here thinking I'd like to own it."

"I'm not saying it's without passion," Spark continued valiantly.

We looked at the painting for a while. Sam's thumb polished the head of the little scholar. I thought about the weird things you find in comic books—Lex Luthor, True Love, Conan the Barbarian. Clarity is at the heart of all things. But right now, I couldn't hear it. I could only hear, through the open window, the certainty of the rain, dulling and rearranging the world. It was intermission and the scene was shifting.

If Johnny came into the living room right now with his easy tread and his smile and his energy, with the solid earth of his being—all that would change. Reality, for me, was in Johnny's presence. That was the truth. For a while. I thought I just needed to come home to be right again, but that's not it. No, no. I have to endure this. I have to endure my own separation. I could imagine many things, but I could not imagine being without Johnny. And yet, that was what I must do.

We looked at the paintings, Spark and I, but Sam's hand was now weighing the scholar. He laid three books on their sides to hold up the shelf and hefted the bookend.

"I wonder what Johnny'd take for these," he said.

Spark stood back from the wall and stretched out her arms toward her own painting. As if holding a brush she began to dab the air, retouching the canvas, making changes here and there; she blocked off an edge with her arm, she added more paint to one side. Then she paused and chewed on a finger.

"I wonder," she said.

Deep inside me, like a wave threatening to break, there was laughter.

"Johnny," I said, standing and crushing my Styrofoam cup from the top down, "he's crazy about those things. You might have to try again next year, Sam."

"I just never seem to have room enough in one painting to say what I want to say," said Spark.

I said, "You don't conform to a living room wall, Spark. You change it all around. You force too much change. For most people."

The laughter was like a great curl inside me. The joke was on me, I was convinced, but it was still worthwhile. My laughter was going to break the bank. It was going to be like the cannons at the end of the symphony. It wasn't going to happen for a while yet, but the promise was there.

When the three of us drifted back outside, I almost heard myself sizzle in the rain. I was a volcano heating up. Johnny's girlfriend had long brown hair and an intelligent face. She was a tall woman, an Amazon, no doubt supremely athletic. His arm rested on her shoulder and his long fingers curved easily into her hair.

But I happened to notice her head turn away. She watched a car pass the house. Her eyes, at a moment that called for repose, seemed instead to be aware of some distraction, betrayed some inner music of doubt.

The tarpaulin above my head held a pool of water. I put my hand up and poked it so a pocket of water splashed out onto a small table of toys, drenching a tin Greyhound bus. After all, I was very pleased to be here. Just when I expect the page to fall and the book to close, I thought, it begins again, and again.

Taking It Plain

Through smoke in the air and an inch of smoky golden Scotch in a crystal glass that must have weighed a pound, I stared at the woman behind the oyster bar. Her black apron sashed over a slim waist and flat stomach drew my attention first. Then I noticed her hair, gleaming brown, that fell into her eyes when she bent her head to dig a knife into the hinge of an oyster. She'd toss her hair back right after setting the half shell and its little offering onto the bed of shaved ice.

Shining brown hair falls. Smile, or grimace, of concentration. Knife screws at the hinge of the shell, knife gripped in a black glove, glove revealing a forearm taut as a cable. Oyster finds its place on the ice. Hair tossed back. She smiles at a customer, reaches for another oyster.

She wore a big white shirt, starched white sleeves pushed above her elbows.

Her smile was shy, half-secretive, as if she were remembering endearments, or hiding trinkets in a birthday cake.

The main thing was the spark of life in her gestures. Hair falls in a spark of light from the chandelier. Smooth, brown ribbon of hair, like the softness inside a dog's ear. Right elbow goes out to a provocative angle, wrist digs at oyster, left arm lays oyster gently down. Hair tossed back. Face revealed. Dark-eyed, shining. She sucked in her cheeks as she reached for another.

Over and over, with minute variations.

Among the people at my table, academics from the university in the twilight of their productive years, was one visiting author, the reason for our get-together. He had spoken earlier that night on campus, invited to Juneau as part of a tour for his magnificent book, a memoir of his work as a marine scientist in the North Pacific. The book included a horrific account of the pollution he had observed and had been unable to arrest. The book was a regional bestseller; his talk was moving, powerful. But at this dinner he was turning out to be a shy and soft-spoken man, one of those individuals who are accomplished and tongue-tied at the same time. The other professors took over the conversation, and despite the presence of our illustrious guest, the dinner-table talk limped through familiar territory. I quit following it and gave myself license to gaze intermittently at the oyster shucker. I wanted to know her name. I wanted to receive one of her oysters, although I had never eaten such a thing in my life.

I leaned toward the author and said, indicating the oyster bar, "Do you think those are safe to eat?"

He watched her for a few moments.

"How could they not be?" he murmured.

"She's very deft," I said.

"There are contests for that sort of thing," he said. "World champions, and so on."

We agreed that she exuded the confidence and grace of a record-holder.

"Shall we try a few?" he said softly, at last. Did he not love the sea and everything in it? What had he come to Alaska for, if not to approach the source?

As the two of us moved up toward the oyster bar, I felt like a high school boy approaching the homecoming queen, stepping near a goddess. Two shy middle-aged men sidling toward the light.

Plates in hand we picked out golden shrimp and sushi rolls, bold enough choices in former days. Then we reached the oysters.

She was lovely up close. Below each cheekbone, dimples the size and shape of a quarter on edge.

"How are these supposed to be eaten?" asked the author.

"Take it plain," she said, pausing in her shucking and leaning toward him. "I like them plain. Or squeeze lemon all over it, and put on a bit of this red sauce. Let it slide down. Take several. You'll want several. We fly these up from the San Juan Islands, and these over here are from Prince William Sound. From a bay untouched by oil."

She looked at me.

"Professor Minton," she said.

"Yes."

"I had you for Cold Lands Geography last year. Oh I hope you don't remember me. I dropped out. Not because I didn't like the class. I just didn't know what I was doing."

"I've been watching you open those oysters," I said. "You surely do know what you're doing." I didn't want to confess to staring. I wanted to say, your skill is intoxicating. Perhaps she understood, for she sailed on.

"Nothing to it. I've been doing this all my life."

"No kidding," said the author.

"My whole life is seafood," she said, and laughed. Then she tossed her head and gave her soft, overlong bangs an additional shove with her gloved arm, revealing the white underside.

"You could win prizes," said the author.

"I have. I'm the fastest oyster shucker on the Northwest Coast two years in a row," she said.

We were in the presence of greatness. Innocence and delight descended upon the two of us, plates in hand.

"I'm sorry I'm no good with names," I began.

"Thank god for that. I'm Ellie Cowan. Enjoy those oysters now. They are the best you can get. The very best."

"Thank you, Ellie."

"Thank you," seconded the author, and we returned triumphant to our table. Where, it turned out, we then had to eat what we had collected. There was a metallic tang and a roar of surf as I ate my first raw oyster, and I quickly followed it with the last of the Scotch.

The truth is, I fell in love. What is it the writer Gorky said, love is like a gay holiday for the heart. And so it was. Not something I would pursue. Just a lovely singing surprise that stayed with me for a week or so. I do not mean that I dropped thirty years and thirty pounds and became a young man again. We were not meant for each other. But why not call it love, after all, if that is what it most resembled? Delight resurfaced.

I would not have wanted anyone to hurt her.

Ellie Cowan. Thinking hard, I thought I remembered, from a year ago, an exchange similar to the one at the oyster bar—a dark-haired woman student sighing, smiling, shoving back her hair, deprecating herself. And looking around at my office, where she had come to collect my signature on her withdrawal slip. She came to face the music and stayed a few minutes out of frank and harmless curiosity to inspect my office décor. I recalled a pleasant sensation of being softly, persistently invaded by her curiosity. It was too early in the semester to have a sense of her strength as a student. I felt neutral about her withdrawal but I wished her good luck as she was leaving—yes, I did try to keep her there a minute longer, with a couple of remarks like that. Good luck to you, Ellie.

Geography is an ancient discipline, but I often feel that I'm making it up. Among Chaucerians and professors of calculus, I always feel like apologizing. Geography is less a subject in itself than a way of looking

46

at humanity's inadequate accommodations to the globe. At one time I wanted to know about every place on this earth—I had a fling with wonderful, youthful greed. I wanted to incorporate the whole planet, make it mine—instead I now teach others to analyze the relationship between humans and their local landscape. What a troubled relationship it is, filled with imperatives, abuses, unexamined traditions, and here and there, incremental gains in understanding.

The proper study of mankind is man, Pope said. Maybe because he said it so well, in rhyme, I can't forget that. I believe he was right. Ultimately, it seems pathetic that we can't study anything without invading it, changing it, and finally studying our own havoc. Which is where we should have started. And, certainly, the havoc is interesting.

Pessimism is common in middle age. How do you reopen Pandora's box? That's what we want to do. Reopen the box.

After six years in Juneau I moved to the main research campus of the University of Alaska up in Fairbanks. At first I felt very far away from all things familiar, though as a geographer, of course, I knew exactly where I was. Indeed one could say I inhabited the center of the known universe. I determined to get to know Fairbanks, the interior of Alaska, the windswept floodplain of the Tanana Valley with its three-million-years-in-the-making accrual of windblown loess, its boreal forest, its domes of schist, its semiarid subarctic climate, growing ever so subtly warmer and wetter with each passing year. And of course its wood-dependent, oil-dependent inhabitants.

The grit in the air that August day wasn't windblown loess, it was parking lot grit. It settled in your skin like cold, gray greasepaint.

I never expected to run into Ellie Cowan on the state fairgrounds in Fairbanks. But I thought of her when I walked past a booth featuring Prince William Sound oysters. You couldn't sell Love Canal oysters, but the name Prince William Sound did survive the oil spill of 1989. The name has the sound of human error and even tragedy in it now, but not of filth. Something pure and magnificent survives. A deep current within the Sound's water helped to flush it clean. Broke up the molecules of crude oil and carried them out to the open ocean. The name of the place suggests a fall, that's it, and reconciliation to a new reality. Forever now this place bears our imprint, but we have a second chance because it was not destroyed. And here were oysters from a sea farm, prepared six different ways, and behind the high counter a cheerful brown-haired woman.

But it wasn't Ellie. I stared for a while, then I wandered away.

Under a gazebo a slight, disarming figure was throwing knives. And scimitars. An Armenian character with a line of patter every bit as magnetizing as his motor skills. I stopped, roped in immediately by his charm and the intensity of his eyes. He was controlling the crowd with his eyes and his talk more than anything else. He did not take his eyes off the crowd: he was paying attention to us. There was a cord, a connection, between him and his audience. The transatlantic cable.

When he finished his act he broke the spell only by turning away, opening his storage trunk, and starting to repack his weapons. The crowd, bereft, remained in place a few moments before accepting dismissal. A woman next to me was handing crackers to the baby on her back, one after the other, and staring at the knife thrower. The baby sucked and gummed its biscuits, looked around, eyeballed the old man next to her. The woman remained oblivious to her child except for the hand that reached back, periodically, loaded with cracker.

Something familiar and graceful about her arm and her profile.

Then she shrugged, as if to rid herself of the knife thrower's influence, turned to the side, and looked at me. Her face was gray and flat, as mine must have been, this cold and gritty afternoon. There was grit in her hair, but her eyes fell on me like candles. Long dimples appeared with a quick smile.

"Oysters," I said, blurting out a memory, and immediately feeling ridiculous.

"Dr. Minton, it's you. What a show. Did you see this show? Could anyone ever do anything as good?"

She gazed at me with fervor. Demanding that I agree. Waiting. I wanted to say some things never change, and lift away from her face brown hair that had gone too long without a cut. "Well," I said helplessly.

"No," she said, "you didn't see." And her eyes filled with tears.

For a second I did not know what to do. I thought, simply look back.

My hands wanted to caress the rolled up sleeves of her faded, flannel shirt. Anything to get back in control. Somehow I managed not to touch, just to look, to let her eyes stop me.

"Oh, I'm so moved by this," she said at last.

"Why don't you go up and tell him," I said. "Shake his hand. Go ahead, he would like it."

"I don't want to bother him, or be a pain. Or be disappointed," she said.

"He'll be thrilled. Nothing to lose. I'll follow."

With that, she did. She ventured toward the little wooden stage—not so shy, after all. Not at all. She gripped the knife thrower's hand with her own broad, equally skilled one, and they spoke to each other with smiles, two equals.

She came back to me, beaming. She let a few of the tears fall, sniffed a bit, and wiped her nose with a wadded tissue from her jeans pockets.

"It's not just him," she said. "It's one thing after another. And here you are in Fairbanks. Somehow I've always remembered your class. I dropped a lot of classes. I don't remember them all."

"And this is your child."

"This is Jenn, my youngest. Is her nose running terribly? Oh I'm so embarrassed. Could you please?"

She handed me a bandanna and I wiped the child's face. Jenn gazed at me with nothing of her mother in her pale blue eyes.

"Ellie," I said, "could I buy you a piece of pie?"

"Oh," she said. "What do you think? Would it be all right?"

She had the nervousness of someone who had been living in confusion for a while. I thought, maybe with a little bit of patronizing, that she needed reminding of good things, soothing things. But the thought that I could soothe her a little felt good. I lifted the backpack while she slithered out of it and unencumbered turned to face me and take her child back.

"Blueberry," she said.

"Make it two, please, with ice cream," I said to the woman in the Lions pie booth.

We sat down at a picnic table beneath a gritty spruce tree and ate warm, tangy blueberry pie, full of the taste of the hills and the wild. Animals eat well, in Alaska, if they eat blueberries. We ate without saying much. The baby, who could stand but not walk, propped herself against the bench and received ice cream from her mother a bite at a time. They looked at each other and laughed, their faces and expressions feeding off each other. Ellie wiped away ice cream after every bite.

She had gone from Juneau to Bristol Bay with her husband, she told me. She had gone from the oyster bar at Juneau's four-star restaurant back to seafood processing without a complaint because that was what she had always done. From the bit of stage she occupied in the city to the assembly line. Things had not worked out. She didn't know why, she said, but I knew.

It was a lifeline to her, an audience. Like the knife thrower, she loved having people watch her perform, and she watched them back, with care and attention and gratitude. When that lifeline was cut and she disappeared into a row of women in aprons cutting up seafood, no matter how much money she made, no matter what she came home to, no matter where she lived, she lived without the secret thing she enjoyed. And she could never, never in a million years have said *This small thing I must have.*

She left her husband because they had become cruel to each other. Neither one knew how it happened. But I knew, because it's my line of work too, holding people's attention. It's a small thing. Every such connection is slender, elusive, but a spark moves along it that keeps people alive.

"What a mess my girl is," she said fondly, after the last spoonful of melted ice cream mixed with warm blueberry filling made contact with her baby's smile. "I feel much better. I must have really needed that pie."

"She certainly likes ice cream."

"All Alaska children like ice cream. Any time of the year. We eat more ice cream than any other state, Dr. Minton, don't you know that?"

She cleaned the little girl emphatically, temporarily flush with confidence again. She pulled out the baby's waistband and stuck a finger into her diaper.

"Still clean for now, you precious," she cooed to the baby, then looked at me. "Would you mind helping me load her back up?"

"Certainly."

Then, for a few seconds, Ellie's gaze rested in mine. Her face wore an expectant but calm expression, as though she were waiting for something to happen, and she would be content to wait as long as it took. Her eyes were very dark. For a minute I wondered if she were assessing me. My body wondered. As if there were no emotion between us—suddenly we were free of that—but pure assessment. And it was the most exciting moment of my summer, to be looked at that way. She looked down for a minute at her child and when she looked back, it was with a smile and raised eyebrows and a full return of ordinary social graces.

"Ready? She's not a lightweight."

I held the backpack and she filled it with Jenn, sticking the child's legs through the holes, pulling them down by the ankles.

"How do you think you'll like Fairbanks, Dr. Minton?"

That was not the question I expected.

"I'm Stanley," I said, and quickly added, "Fairbanks is very interesting."

"The kids and I are here for now," she said, "and we'll make the best of it, eh Jenn? Up you go. Now I have to round up my boys from the midway, um, Stanley."

"Please. I hope I see you again, Ellie."

"I expect you will," she said, not risking my first name again, and gave me a wide grin that made both dimples appear like a frame to her smile.

I held the pack and she turned her back to me, and put one arm then another through the straps. She made the straps comfortable on her shoulders and I finally let the pack frame settle.

"I'm glad I ran into you," I said.

"I can always use a piece of blueberry pie," she said. "Until next time," and she waved and turned away, while I remained planted, watching this mobile creature bear her complicated burden past me. She moved toward the midway.

In the distance beyond her, a ride called the Slingshot catapulted two young people into the sky. They would fall back down the extent of bungee-type cables, bounce up, and fall down until the energy in the cables was spent. At this hour you would expect twilight in a more southern city. But right here the sun, nowhere in evidence behind low clouds, was a long way from setting.

Facing the Music

Annie Roosa and I knew each other for a couple of years before we found ourselves snowbound in Koyukuk and spent the night together. I hoped it could become a regular thing. But she thought no, it wasn't good enough for either one of us. She thought my silence afterward signaled a lack of interest. I was stunned. As if when change as overwhelming as a new season and a shift in the weather floods hollow, dying cells with hope, you're supposed to follow it up with words, lots of words, or lose it. Instead of lying there, aghast and sated at the same time, you're supposed to grab the microphone and give a speech. The more she wanted captions and comments, the more I disappointed her, receding from her like someone going the wrong way down the walkway at the airport. Making an appearance, then reversing direction, getting smaller, getting back into the plane. One of us went from passion to disappointment in just two nights; the other didn't even know what hit him.

So we went back to being friends. Of a sort, anyway. I have a little flight service and she was always flying around Alaska to one village or another, to one funeral or another, so we saw each other on the job so to speak. I'd fly her from Fairbanks to Allakaket and two days later to Galena and then back to Fairbanks. I care for her in a special way I'd rather not think too much about.

Annie was an alcoholism counselor for the Interior Native Association. She taught classes and set up meetings and tried to coordinate all those services that INA extended to the villages. Annie covered a territory the size of North Dakota. For me, a pilot, weeks spent going from point to point in this bountiful space of forest, mountain, and valley is exactly right—this is what I want out of life. But for her, no. I think the job was hard on her. Not the flying, but the hopelessness of it. All those scattered generations in this huge country, what could she offer them?

This time in Koyukuk. It was late in the day. I went up to the little ticket shack I shared with half a dozen other charter services to do a little paperwork after the blowing snow grounded my flight. I was trying to give up smoking in those days. I leaned against the counter and then decided to do an isometric exercise against it, and pretty soon I decided to shove the damn thing off its bolts and across the room. For some few seconds it seemed like I might succeed, like the Incredible Hulk, might actually rip those bolts out and destroy the place, when the door slammed and Annie Roosa's voice said, "What are you doing, Penn?"

When I turned around she said, "God, you look awful."

I gave in to a moan, sort of a bellow. "I want a smoke," I said, and she laughed and reddened and opened up her arms to me.

Withdrawal, I mean from addiction, was a subject she knew something about after all, but she didn't have to rescue her pilot—she could laugh at him. It must have felt good. She compensated for her cruel laughter with a long, warm, sexy hug. One thing led to another. Our knees got weak, holding each other. We kind of collapsed together down behind that counter. We lay there fully clothed and breathless for several minutes. Then she raised herself above me, her left hand on my belt, and looked at me with that careless joy you have when lust is new and mutual, and she whispered, "Come on over to where I'm staying. It's nice and warm." While she was talking she pulled my shirt out and let her fingers massage my skin and I lay there and suffered her whims until she said, "Come with me," and pulled me up and we ran through the snow to her toasty hideaway. It had a blazing woodstove, snowshoes on the wall, oilcloth on the table, everything you dream about as a kid when you're dreaming about being a bush pilot in Alaska. And a woman, flushed, embarrassed, hungry, seeing in you what you see in her.

I guess maybe we were together again once in Fairbanks in her apartment—she called the place luxurious. Wall to wall carpet and hot running water and a nice view of the sky, plus a bedroom for her daughter who spent most of the year at boarding school down in Sitka. We spent the night in her apartment and that morning when I actually spoke, when I said, "See you tonight?" she answered fast, "Oh, Penn, I don't think so. This isn't the right thing for us. Can't you tell? If we stop now, we can still have our friendship, can't we?"

So it wasn't mutual anymore. What could I do but take her word for it.

I guess that was a few years ago. Still I felt funny when she came into my Fairbanks office not long ago and we got to talking and she told me, with a few giggles, how she had connected with a masseur recently at Tolovana Hot Springs. I wanted to hear the story, and I liked to see her face suffused with the pleasure of it. Still, I felt provoked. Even territorial, after all this time.

Annie was just over fifty, and I knew she had a rose tattooed on her shoulder, and I knew she'd have looked like a hot rose in that tub at Tolovana. A hot pink rose surrounded by steam and snowdrifts. Blonde head, one breast, one long red scar. Shoulders that fit my hands. (Was I supposed to tell her that? *Your shoulders are like birds in my hands?*)

Tolovana Hot Springs is a primitive place in the mountains north of Fairbanks. To get there, you have to snowmachine, cross-country ski, or hike eleven rugged miles, from a small turnout on the Elliott Highway over a windswept dome. At the springs are two cabins with propane cookstoves; a spring-fed hot tub sits next to an icy creek. The spring is hot but the creek is cold so there's a rubber hose into the tub from the creek, which allows you to temper the water whenever you get too warm. They snowmachined in, Annie and a friend from her AA group—like most rehab counselors, Annie came to her job from her own experience—and joined a half dozen or so other people out there. That's how it works: someone reserves the two cabins for a couple of days and invites a small crowd. Once you've hauled in your supplies, you've got it made: nothing to do but soak, eat, talk, ski the long low valley, smoke and drink if you've a mind to. Of course these people wouldn't have been doing that.

As Annie talked, my mind lingered on the details that she didn't provide. Her shoulders, her hips, her breathless little co-dependent laugh as she tried to fit in and make herself good company to five or six strangers. Her pale hair frosting around her face, because the air is so cold. And then the flush of excitement because even though she gave up drinking years ago, with Annie any kind of party, the stimulation, the flow of it, worked a toxic effect. Stone cold sober and drug free, she'd still give you the impression she was flying.

The edge of Annie was right out there. She attracted guys who wanted to protect her and guys who wanted to beat her. She could fall either way; you always sensed that. During the years I knew her she always took the right path, she did the thing that she had to do, but it often felt like a close call.

Maybe that was why I wanted to spend more time with her. I must have liked it, that vulnerability. That night in Koyukuk, our night, she showed me her charcoal drawings of Native kids and the little totems she carried with her when she traveled—potbellied goddesses, Sheila-na-gigs, carvings of naked women. Her talismans. Every day during that week, years ago, she had attended the burial of another young man or woman she knew. Once three twelve-year-olds, who broke open a barrel of methanol they found on the beach.

I didn't understand. I could not inhabit Annie's way of thinking. Annie could draw, she could paint, she had a BFA from the Pratt Institute in Brooklyn. She wanted to retire early and go into art therapy. She loved art and art loved her back; it was good for her. So why alcoholism counseling, why this losing battle? I have a theory, sure. I figure she went into counseling because, and this is heartless of me, here comes the cold fish—I figure it was the easiest thing to do. Her own experience gave her the credential and the contacts. The job paid well. And she cared, of course she did. But it was also the course of least resistance. At least, that's what I used to think. Maybe there's more to it. Maybe there are things that call to you. Not wilderness but a human voice. I don't know.

I could feel it—she didn't need to tell me—that Annie was inhabited by demons. One of them a Monster Controller she couldn't get rid of. Every day was a war: Annie and her love for the world, a whorish love with no limits, against Annie the Monster Controller, the self-hater. She told me herself where her breast cancer came from; she had some theory about her tissue turning against her. I didn't like to hear her talk that way. Maybe that was the day she took silence for disinterest.

Annie carried memories like spurs she'd use against herself. Things bothered her. Two ex-husbands back East, and after all this time she still hated to think of herself as having betrayed them and having harmed her kids with her own instability. She claimed to have a history of leaving people. I'd call it a few unfortunate investments. Are you not allowed, Annie, to learn from your own mistakes?

At Tolovana Hot Springs, she said, getting into her story, she found herself one of five naked strangers neck-deep in hot spring water, victorious after an eleven-mile journey through blowing snow over Tolovana Dome and down through two miles of spruce forest with headlamps to light the trail. One young woman had walked in, pulling a plastic toboggan loaded with frozen bread dough. She boarded the sled at the top of the last ridge and coasted for the last two miles down to the hot springs, braking with the heels of her Sorels every twenty feet, bread dough between her knees. She set out the loaves to rise while she soaked.

The five of them, the five heads shrouded with steam above five naked bodies, politely cast about for conversation and landed on the topic of close encounter with a famous person. Annie's AA buddy reported that his mother had done Al Capone's laundry decades ago in Miami Beach. One woman had lived on the same street as Bennett Cerf. The best story was told by a guy who used to race cars. Once at a race down south he leaned over a gate at a track and caught Paul Newman's eye. The actor was leaning over the same gate, perhaps six feet away. They nodded at each other. Each raised a palm in salute.

"Why didn't you talk to him!" one of the women said.

"This was a place where he enjoyed being one of the drivers, one more car guy. He didn't have to deal with fame. But only if everybody agreed to go along. I wouldn't have wanted to mess it up for him."

Then it was Matt's turn. Matt the itinerant masseur, newly arrived in Alaska. He had hardly spoken up till now.

"I met Mother Teresa's cook," he began shyly.

The audience approved and asked for more.

"She gave a lecture on vegetarian cooking at a conference," he continued. "Well, vegetarian—it was called something like Eating with a Saint, or What does a Saint Eat?"

"What do saints eat?" someone asked.

"Root vegetables," said Matt. "Mostly."

"What was the conference about?"

"Healing."

"There's so much healing going on these days," said the race car driver.

"Maybe that word is all the rage," Annie had blurted out, suddenly ruffled, irritated, there in the hot tub. "But the situation doesn't change."

She was instantly ready to go to bat for healers. Then she paused, realizing that she was about to defend Matt. Assuming again. Rushing to the defense of a quiet, gentle person who had asked for nothing.

"What doesn't change?" Matt asked her. With interest. His eyes, she thought, or the shape of his face.

"That people hurt," she said. "That people are walking around traumatized. Oh, damn. Here I go again. Who wants to talk like this? I'm not at work now, and I'm not going to get into this! But sometimes, I think, what could be more important?"

The two of them went skiing together the next day, gliding through the woods in the creek bottom. He looked comical in his ski garb, Value Village purchases. She was amused at his appearance—big head and long arms, chunky torso, awkwardness on borrowed skis, those warm brown eyes, with, she said, "that yellow light, that look." It seemed to her Matt was looking at something about her that she herself had long forgotten.

His skills as a healer were put to use that night. One of the party, a musher, came around a hairpin curve in the woods too fast. The front of his dogsled hit a tree—he fell over the handle and severely bruised a rib. Matt tended him while the others made pork burritos and sliced the fresh bread, swirled with apricots and almonds. Annie felt buffered from all harsh realities: the extraordinary luxury of the hot water, the good food, the remoteness, and their very own on-site medical help. It seemed too good to be true, she told me.

She and her snowmachining buddy, Al Hurley from AA, rode past Matt the next morning on their way out. He was happily struggling up toward the summit with skis over his shoulder. He stopped walking and gazed at her, basking in her outrageous smile. She didn't know or care at that moment if she'd see him again.

But two days later he knocked at her door in Fairbanks. She opened it and there he stood, arms full of salmon—one huge fish wrapped in paper. "Will you accept a fish?" he asked. There was no doubt what he was really asking. She knew too that she was being asked to invite a gypsy into her life. This man was jobless and homeless both. She stood back and held the door wide.

She warmed to her narrative and her skin glowed. Matt, she said, knew how to massage her feet so as to relieve collateral pain from her recent mastectomy, pain that manifested in her shoulder. She seemed to accept his knowledge of the human body as being akin to a medical degree. And that fish. She went on about the fish in his arms and what it led to, as though I'd never heard of symbols and metaphors and sex and God. As though I hadn't slept with her myself. With a laugh she informed me that, past fifty and post-cancer, "it all still works!" There's one word to describe the way she talked. When she said, "It all still works," I'd have to say she caroled.

"At my age," she went on.

"Just say the word, Annie. At your age and mine."

"Oh, Penn. We're good friends, you and I."

"Of course we are. I'm happy for you."

Still her masseur took some getting used to, on my part.

He drove a Geo, a worthless car. A dodgem, a bumper car. They shouldn't let those cars outdoors. When he'd go out into the hills scouting for a cabin, Annie fretted over him, driving that car. He summoned up behavior that, I thought, she had outgrown. Taking care of guys in worthless cars, I mean.

When I found myself meditating on her private life this way I didn't know what to make of it. It bewildered me. After all her years of counseling others, here she was embracing that very same moral exchange that sets people back. At least I saw it as an exchange. Matt Giatti gets a warm and comfortable place to live, all expenses paid, and Annie gets a man to sleep with, to fuss over. That part of the exchange was on the surface, it was obvious. But deep within her, the place inside where she opened the door to a fish, well it was off-limits to me, but there was some kind of exchange going on there, too. I didn't like it that I begrudged Annie her pleasure. I tried to stay with that idea for awhile: what's really bothering you, Penn, why do you feel like someone's moving in on you? Can't you let someone live her own life?

I went over it in my head the way I go over incidents in flight. I inventory it and look dispassionately at everything I did and log it all down. That should work, in life as in flying. Because they're the same thing. A negotiation with forces out there, a stay. And a successful flight is a clean and simple thing.

She still had to finish a course of radiation therapy. And she decided to leave Alaska to get it.

"Matt and I," she yelled at me over the engine noise, on our way home from Huslia, several weeks later, "we're going home for awhile."

"Home, Annie?"

"Thunder Bay, Ontario. I'm going to get the radiation there. I can be with my mother. I'm really happy about it. This cancer has helped me change my life, Penn. I'm finally somebody who can make a decision. I'm going to be quitting this job at last. I'm not doing this anymore," and she waved her hand generally at the window, meaning she wasn't going to keep stitching at the rescue net, wasn't going to keep throwing herself back out there with it, season after season.

Leaving Alaska.

I went to Annie's apartment the next week to say good-bye, taking an expensive box of the watercolor crayons I knew she liked and a new sketchbook. Matt was moving around the place packing. An average-sized guy, in pretty good shape for a man our age. A big sort of mashed face, a friendly self-possessed look to him. He left us alone to talk as if he knew that Annie and I had a shared history.

Annie's apartment, a third floor suite in a big block put up to meet the housing boom brought by the oil industry, was as sunny and bright as you could get in Fairbanks. A picture window made it seem as if the living room were floating in air. Annie, cross-legged on the sofa, seemed smaller than ever and spoke breathlessly like someone swimming. Her skin—those places where age appears, her chin, her neck, her arms—seemed to tremble. I couldn't find the outline of her body there in the living room next to me. Age, or cancer, had brought a new kind of vulnerability.

Matt asked if we were hungry and brought in plates of stir-fried noodles. Salmon, peapods, peppers, and Japanese noodles. No root vegetables. I wondered if this was that very salmon. The fish that opened the door. Annie liked watching him move, and I could see why—he gave every gesture its due. He moved at his own steady pace. All right, the man was easy to take. He probably did Tai Chi. I wouldn't put it past him.

I told them a little about my own venture Outside, three years ago. How I tried to set up shop near my family in Michigan, but couldn't bear it, couldn't leave Alaska after all. How my own sour personality got in my way in Michigan—up here, I didn't have to pretend—there was room for a guy like me up here. I couldn't explain it, but I knew then, loneliness and all, that I had to come back here and, as I plainly put it, "face the music." I'm okay here, even without my family, my sister and ex-wife, the kids.

"Face the music," Matt said. "I try to do that."

I thought, you do? You've sure been lucky so far. "How's that?" I said politely.

"It's an invitation," he said, "to look more closely." He moved his chopsticks around in the black china bowl. Ate the last bite. "You want to front the experiences that come your way. Face the music. You want to watch the score, see." He reached out a hand for Annie's bowl and rose to his feet.

"Yeah, I like that," he continued. It was as though he'd never heard the cliché before.

Annie smiled at me as if to say—Isn't he the greatest?

At the door I kissed her and she hugged me back. "Say something archetypal, Annie," I said. "Give me a word of advice."

She didn't bat an eye. "Penn, what I've got is my experience and my faith," she said without hesitation. "That's what I rely on, in everything. If I do that, I always have what I need. I've put my life in your hands a couple dozen times and you've never let me down. I have faith in you."

It was only a month later that I walked unthinkingly across my kitchen with the TV schedule in my hand to answer the phone, and Alvin Hurley said, "Penn. Do you have the news about Annie?"

"Well, they were on their way to Thunder Bay, last I..."

"They got there. Got there fine. Her sister called me yesterday. Annie's died of a heart attack. Three days ago. In her mother's arms."

I didn't believe it. He had to repeat the news. In her mother's arms, he said, with determination.

"Did you know," he added, "her real name was Anya. She was Estonian. I only knew her a little bit, I see that now. But still..."

"Yeah. Yeah," I said. I realized through my feeling of unreality that Al was in grief, that he could use my help. I tried to hang on a little bit, let him talk, say something. But I didn't believe him. I had to get off the phone and sit there for an hour and replay his words in my mind over and over.

I blame the job. I blame whatever lashed Annie to stay with that job. Maybe that "collateral pain" in her shoulder was a warning of heart trouble, maybe she should have paid attention to it, not let it get massaged away by the clever hands of a self-proclaimed healer. Now another voice in my head says, surely, receiving tender care in the last summer of her life isn't what killed Annie. I can't be sure.

The roaring in her ears was so loud. All those people in pain and she knew the peculiar nature of that pain so well, she knew about drowning in that river. She didn't know what was happening in her own body.

When a person dies they no longer exist except in someone's love for them. I loved her. Maybe lots of people did. Well, she didn't want my love, and for what it's worth, I didn't think too much of Matt Giatti's;

it wouldn't have lasted. But as it turned out lasting wasn't necessary. Lasting was not part of the exchange.

I miss her exuberance, her excess of energy, and not only that I miss the thing that killed her. Her love for the people she served, those miserable alcoholics and wife-beaters, those drinkers in the bush and their hopelessness and their hope. They didn't ask her to sacrifice her life. I don't blame them. It was her love. Her love didn't exist in the sky, it existed right here on this earth. I miss her love. I want that kind of love in my life. I don't know how to get it, how to ask for it, how to open my door to a fish.

Last week I landed in the village of Talchaket with a load of groceries for the trading post and a pile of other things as well, and Johnny Carew came out of the small terminal building to help me unload the order. The village was somewhat deserted otherwise; a hangover morning, I sometimes thought, when villages were quiet like this. I guess Johnny's about thirty, a good looking young man who's an expert heavy equipment driver and works in remote sites most of the summer. I'm always glad to see him. We shifted box after box of soup and chili, tea and pop and crackers onto the loading dock where an all-terrain vehicle would come to collect it. All that was left in the plane were the eight pale blue cases of Calvert's gin.

"Wait a sec, Johnny," I said, before he bent to reach for one. He leaned on the dolly cart and looked at me.

"Make up your mind, man," he said.

"What in hell am I hauling that stuff for?"

"Well, because you can make a few pennies off the misery of your dusky brethren, like everyone else, Penn," he said.

"Maybe so," I said. We looked at the gin and at each other. I thought, is that true? "Although, wait a minute," I added. "You're my dusky brethren."

"Yeah, yeah."

After a minute, I found more to say. "And I care about you."

After a pause, Johnny said, "I know you're serious, Penn, but I don't know how to help you with this one. Although, brother, I don't mind your ugly face either. For what that's worth."

We walked the empty cart back to the loading dock and sat down. Johnny took the crumpled pack of Kools out of his breast pocket and offered me one; I waved it away. He lit up. One of the smells I've always liked. Cigarette smoke, mixing with the faint sour tang of fuel oil, the faint rot of mushrooms around us in the early fall. Smells that add to the fantasy of freedom that led me to this job and this place to begin with.

"The year I gave those up," I said, nodding at the cigarette on his lip, "was the hardest year of my life. Except for one thing. There was this woman. She took pity on me." Johnny grinned. "No, it's true. She had a rose tattooed on her shoulder."

What if I became one of those pilots who wouldn't haul booze. *I don't haul booze,* I thought, imagining myself making the announcement to a customer. There weren't many declarations you could make about Penn DeAngelo. Maybe that would be a first. I imagined a conversation out there about me:

—*Penn DeAngelo doesn't haul liquor.*

—*What, is he a Christian?*

—*No, just doesn't haul booze, one of his things.*

"A woman with a tattoo," Johnny repeated, smiling. "Tattooed Rosie."

"She was a woman with experience," I said. "Let me tell you. And faith. So she said, and I believed her." Johnny raised his hand to remove his cigarette; I could see in his fine hand how young he really was. His skin was smooth as caramel, the black hair on his upper lip barely enough to shave. I didn't know what to do. The liquor was bought and paid for, and withholding an order was unfamiliar behavior to me. In a few minutes an ATV would come down from the village buzzing like a cloud of mosquitoes. I was happy though, to be carrying Annie around in my heart, like a rose. It made my heart feel big, and painful, and alive. But most of all, this: I was lucky to have Alaska around me still, to smell the cigarette smoke and the dying leaves. So what would happen now? What would happen if I forced a few changes in my life, because of things that I loved?

Johnny took the last drag and flung the cigarette away in a neat arc, like he was expressing mixed feelings of his own, toward this country, toward his own living room. Like the mixed feelings a person always carries toward his own self. To think when I was giving up those things, along came a soft and beautiful woman who found my struggle attractive and endearing and made me spend the night with her. Have I ever once said thank you for that night? Instead I met her love with my half smile and my silence, and when it was over with a sour shrug.

I really ought to try something new.

"I gotta shift that stuff around a bit, Johnny, so I won't be unbalanced when I take off," I said, and clapped him on the shoulder. "Balance issues. Dangerous thing. Adios, buddy, this fucker's airborne." I walked back to the plane like I had nothing to hide. If you know how to fly a plane—that's a good thing, to fly a plane, a useful thing. It ought to be of some use to people. The sound of a plane above a village ought to make people happy inside, not be a prelude to nightmare. I better not think too much about this. I won't find what I'm looking for if I try to reason it out. Just go with the impulse. Side with the angels, for a change. Don't even tell anyone.

"Where's our gin?" they'll ask Johnny.

Johnny could handle it. "Don't know. Didn't say. That's DeAngelo. Maybe it'll be coming later. Give you a hand loading this stuff?"

Aurora Borealis

The sky ever-present
even in darkness beneath the skin.
　　　—Wisława Szymborska, "The Sky"

Leslie Talus lay on her side, knees pointed at her chin, her body forming a question mark under the fluffy quilt. Her eyes in the dark bored holes toward the clock radio. At 2:00 AM she would rise, pull on snowpants and parka, and head out into the frigid night to see the meteor shower. If the sky were to fill with falling stars, if heaven were to blaze tonight, she intended to show up. Like an obedient student rewarded with a new challenge, she intended to be there, a blank slate, an open book for the lesson.

She lay with one arm over her legs, skin to skin, muscle to muscle. She told herself, "Shut your eyes. Go to sleep, you weary hobo. Let the stars drift slowly by." Her knees pressed closer to the emptiness inside. It was always there. Like an old friend, like a hitchhiker she couldn't get rid of: that desert space, the defining gap that was the true and secret reality of Leslie Talus—author, professor, lover, madwoman, drunk. Not one of those characters more true than another. The truth was the hole inside. But days would go by now, and she wouldn't feel the emptiness, wouldn't know it. If she were to turn off the alarm now, roll over and sleep for a good eight hours, she wouldn't be facing it now, either. Wouldn't be hugging that hole inside with its memory of sharp edges.

But if she didn't rise at two, she'd miss the meteor shower.

She didn't want to miss any event in the northern sky. Her sabbatical year was one-third over. So far, so good. She had put together a good routine at the University of Alaska. Four to eight hours of research and writing. An hour of lifting weights in the gym, and she could feel the results even now, in her bare arm that lay over her thighs and her knees. The extra muscle was helping her keep warm, helping her to face the cold. And the blackness! Three hundred and fifty miles to the sea, in three directions: three hundred and fifty miles of unbroken snow, of forty below, of a silence like thunder. Maybe the creaking of a tree or the sound of a snow machine, but all the squabbling, fighting families were locked inside on nights like this, keeping their angry voices, their fear, their desperation, their eagerness to pull the skin off one another, keeping all of that indoors, away from her, locked away from the silence. The snow rolled on unbroken and no one could see it, either, under the dark sky. Blackness left to itself. A landlocked land.

Leslie forced herself outside into that blackness every night at 11:00 PM for one half hour at least before bed. Before she allowed herself to climb onto her inflatable mattress and burrow under the down quilt, she dressed in long underwear and down pants and parka and went outside in search of the northern lights. She hadn't been two weeks in Alaska, back in September, asking residents about the lights, when she realized that most people here never made an effort to see them, to compare displays, to know what was really going on above them at night when they slept or when they argued or when they sat numb in front of the TV. It was like living at a beach and not going down to the water every morning to see what the tide brought in. Leslie had never lived at the beach, but she had always imagined she would do that—like getting the newspaper or checking the mail; you'd do it every day at the same time if you lived in such a place. Here in Fairbanks the weather was always in your face, getting under your collar, the weather was in search of you. There was no getting away from the weather, no ignoring it.

You could cower, though. You could huddle inside, give it the victory. Or you could go into it. Walk into it with some goal in mind. Her goal was the aurora borealis. She would keep a record. She would look every night. A directive to herself. A life-giving routine. Every night at eleven, no matter what: one half hour's stroll to the top of the ridge from her fourplex and back, eyes on the sky.

And already, by the middle of November, she knew more about the aurora than most Alaskans she had met so far. If they weren't avid hobbyists of the phenomena, they treated it like a bit of the backdrop, gave it the importance of, say, the price of broccoli. The appearance of seasonal fruit at the supermarket. Worth two minutes of conversation.

But Leslie had been astonished. And filled with joy the first time she saw the performance of the aurora.

On campus, back in September, she had been given this one-bedroom apartment in a fourplex. She brought her possessions in from the trunk of the Buick like a nomad setting out pillows and samovar: the inflatable bed from the Healthy Balance catalog, the goose-down quilt, a box of books, two plastic crates of files and notes, the laptop, a whistling tea kettle. No photographs, no inspirational sayings decoupaged on little plaques. The sole décor would be the view from the plate glass living room window. A ridge covered in gold and green, the spheres and arrows of birch and spruce, curved to the left like a protecting arm around a boggy plain of black spruce and a few old hay fields, which in September were filled with cranes and wild geese. Hundreds, thousands of them. Lifting and wheeling and settling. Then they were gone and the sky turned milky with the threat and promise of snow, the gold faded from the trees. The sunsets and sunrises were like torches blazing at a primitive ritual, long and spectacular.

When the snow came, it stayed. From the first snowfall the world turned white.

Leslie reserved a carrel in the library and set up her work station. At the supermarket she exulted at the price and availability of salmon and halibut. She filled a cupboard with a library of herbal teas, one to match every wince, every bruise, internal and external, as if she were royalty and not allowed to suffer. None of them comforted the hole inside. But she had learned how to set that one at bay: set a clock, build a routine, follow your body forward.

Let the demons see what good care someone is taking of this person, Leslie Talus.

After the first night of aurora-watching, she made a date with herself to walk outside every night at eleven, and more often than not the aurora kept faith with her. A pale spooky green scarf most of the time, one night he became a centaur, his legs eating up the sky. She was so amazed she fell over into the snow. Here was a light in the sky you could stare at unshielded. Under the gay streamers of his performance, she laughed out loud. The hole inside became a laugh, curling up within, bigger and bigger. Leslie had never felt such a peculiar relief from such a faraway source. She couldn't make sense of it. The best she could do was say goodnight after an hour, and remember to show up the next night. She carried the experience like a secret that made her skin glow.

When she was younger, an undergraduate at Rice, taking philosophy and economics for the first time, she used to have the most delightful and acute sensation that previously closed-off rooms in her brain were being unlocked, air was rushing through. There was power up there. Ceilings were raised. She would look up from Wittgenstein just to enjoy the sensation of oxygen rushing through new pathways in her head.

Leslie believed fervently that human beings tended to shut down, as if to conserve energy—God knows where the tendency came from, but there it was. We don't use all of our mental capacity. Instead we creep along like a minimalist version of ourselves. Even people who weren't in the grip of depression were subdued, sedated, as if by default somehow. Even a healthy person needed to take action to become more fully alive.

But Leslie had learned in the past that the driver's seat was illusory. Only when her whole body, never her mind alone, engaged in a pursuit, could she have any reasonable faith she wouldn't crash. For one thing she could not select her thoughts. There was no gatekeeper, no one in charge, keeping this, storing that, jettisoning something else. Thoughts unbidden, unexpected, like leftovers in a neglected refrigerator, troubled her constantly. Softened carrots, rock-hard lemons, a little green cone of Sap Sago cheese that's been in the family for generations. Why do I have to deal with this? she'd ask herself in the midst of a mental harangue. Why am I filthying up my head with these bitter, chewed-up spitballs of monologue. I have a mind like a sewer. I need air, oxygen, ozone!

Change—growth—of the degree she lusted for during this reprieve required full participation of thought, feelings, and body—and maybe something else too. In the meantime the northern lights put her into a routine that she found rewarding. Instead of following my heart, she thought, I'll follow my behavior.

Visiting lecturers and celebrities came and went in the other apartments. Once a Japanese Danish woman, an artist, stayed for two weeks. She painted screens. Leslie invited her over for tea, and the artist reciprocated. Leslie tried to explain about the grandeur, the color, the freedom of the night sky. The artist nodded and responded in English but with such an overwhelming and complex accent that Leslie could barely understand a word. Her speech was like a running brook, mellifluous but indecipherable. Leslie would listen intently for several minutes and realize she had no idea what the woman was saying.

Oddly enough a connection grew between them independent of language.

Leslie would smile and nod, frown or wince, if needed, following the woman's face and tone. Maybe she veered close to duplicity, or maybe she was like a baby, pre-language, watching a friendly adult's face. Maybe neither woman could have sworn in an affidavit as to what their friendship was about, what they shared. It didn't matter. The connection was tangible.

In fact, the deep, dark sound of the artist's voice made a pleasant antiphony to Leslie's writing. By day she chipped away at her research notes, trying to follow one clear and logical sentence with another. Leslie came from a state that had been transformed utterly by Big Oil before she was born, and now she found herself in another. Alaskans, she observed, were in the process of sitting up aghast after having been raped by change, so to speak. The swan of wealth had flown away. And only a few Alaskans, in her opinion, were willing to admit that they had not enjoyed an equal partnership with the oil companies. This was no marriage of peers. The oil companies, she wrote, learned just enough local politics, knew what they could get away with. They learned the tribe's lingo, its greed, its fears. They hired experts in human nature.

From six to eight Leslie lifted weights in the student recreation center and sometimes joined an aerobic dancing group. Back in the apartment she prepared salmon, halibut, or scallops every night. Alaskans had no idea of the luxury in which they lived! A few dollars a pound for pure, wild, magnificent fish! And at eleven she went outside to inspect the dome of the northern sky.

When he did not greet her eyes—when constellations were flung from horizon to horizon or when the sky was muffled with clouds— Leslie felt a surprising pang of abandonment. She remembered what it was like to be filled with dark matter, and she was afraid. Her hopes stood out as pathetic as cardboard cutouts. Even though she stood on a deserted street at midnight, she knew people were turning away from her, in pity and disgust, and ultimately with complete disregard.

Except for those terrible people who saw her as an object. A vessel. A place to stick something.

Her own past, those days when she willingly gave herself to men as an object, those days when she willingly mistook physical touch for connection, came back to her with their weird appeal, and she was shamed.

In the past year, Leslie had relied upon herself for physical pleasure, and a couple of times, as a mental exercise, she had accomplished orgasm without touch. Sitting against the wall, using her mind alone, she reached that amazing place. When I am back with a man, she thought, I might just look up at his face one night in bed and think to myself, "I know for a fact neither you nor I are really necessary," and it'll be my own private joke. He'll think, "What is she laughing at? What's that grin on her face?"

Alaska was her experiment. And perhaps experimentation would keep her above the abyss just a little longer this time.

A few times on her walks she shared the street with a pair of moose, a mother and a calf. The giant, wondrous animals moved in the most peculiar way—as if strung on bungee cords. They moved slowly under imperceptible guidance, awkward.

Campus police had posted a warning about this particular moose family. A few years earlier, a student in Anchorage had been killed right outside the gym on campus by a moose, trampled to death. The moose had been under stress all day from passing students, and it just lashed out. Give them a wide radius, police said, over and over. Leave the bicycle trail if a moose appears in front of you. Don't go around him.

To be threatened by wildlife outside her own apartment! What a wonderful place. Each night Leslie walked a little farther. She took a flashlight and walked on the bike trail, imagining every sound to be a moose. I'm on bungee cords, Leslie thought; I'm on a leash, but I haven't reached its full length yet. And I'm going to act like I'm cured, like I'm free, until I am or know the reason not. Walk as far as I can in my ignorance.

When the Japanese Danish artist left, two women moved in next door: a sculptor, who cut and welded abandoned metal objects into huge outdoor displays, and a horticulturist. They doted on their dog, a big golden shepherd, whose beauty was marred by a startling black muzzle. To Leslie the dog looked as if it had dipped its head in motor oil. It looked a bit like a hyena, in fact; but the women lavished attention, even conversation, on their pet. Leslie frequently took it for walks; fussing over the animal gave her something more to do.

These two women, lovers, blazed at her sometimes like a floor lamp, like an open furnace in fact. Her skin flushed and she wanted to hide. Their lifestyle, their boldness, their comfort with each other, was new to her. They were never preoccupied with the needs of a ghostly husband or ghostly children: they had all that they needed in each other, or close enough. They looked frankly at Leslie with nothing to hide and all the time in the world. She was happy to keep company with the dog and thus establish a marginal connection with the dog's owners. Chola was its name. She had their permission to retrieve it any time, lope off for a half hour or an hour, and release it into the arctic entryway of their apartment at the walk's end. She didn't usually take Chola on her aurora expeditions, though. By then the women and their dog were tucked up in bed. They were early risers, clinging to their own routines. Leslie thought she understood.

One aurora-less midnight she saw the moose near the end of her street. A dense black cut-out, unmistakable. Closer to Leslie under a street lamp a man was writing in a notebook. Could he be a safety officer, or fish and game, writing a citation for the moose? She stopped near him, just outside the pool of light. The moose, twenty feet ahead of them, picked its way slowly over a berm of snow and crossed the street. It turned and walked away, its great muscular haunches rotating above delicate legs; its ankles were narrow as table legs. She stepped a little closer.

He looked at her.

"Dangerous animal," he said. "I've been told."

He was attractive, healthy looking. Somehow his wide, thick glasses made him look reliable. She liked his natty fleece jacket. The jacket suggested nothing more ominous than a trustworthy consumer of trendy clothes.

"Are you out enjoying the wildlife?" he went on. He spoke with an odd accent. His words precise and well spaced, like an organized silverware drawer. Maybe English. Ah, in fact, yes, he was her new downstairs neighbor; she had seen him the night before in that eggplant jacket, leaving at dinnertime with a crowd in a Jeep Wagoneer. Off to a restaurant or potluck somewhere. A brief flash of envy as she watched him shake hands all around and accept the front passenger seat while others crowded in back.

"The moose is amazing, but I am really looking for the northern lights," she said.

"Yes, last night I saw them."

"Incredible."

"You think so?"

"Oh, yes. I'm so gratified to see them! Aren't you? Every night I come out and hunt for them. More often than not, they're up there."

He considered this, while they both stared at the slow-moving animal stepping into the street, heading away from them.

"No, I'm not gratified," he said. "They seemed to me, in a way, like the flags around a used car lot. Getting in the way of the stars, in fact."

American, definitely. The snarl, the trashy metaphor. An American acting like a Brit? Leslie looked him over.

"Well, I've seen stars," she said. "But I never saw the aurora until two months ago. I've gotten to—well—gotten to know it a bit. It gets more interesting, perhaps—the variations."

"I've seen stars myself," he said. "From every hemisphere, but never this far north."

How many hemispheres are there, she wondered. Four or two?

"What takes you to so many hemispheres?" she asked.

"I write books. And you?"

"I write books too. I'm on sabbatical from the University of Oklahoma in Norman. The aftermath of oil dependence, that's my specialty."

He looked less than interested. She didn't mind. She observed herself warming to a challenge. Have some fun with this self-possessed, nicely appointed stranger encountered at a lamppost. Why? Impulse. Old habit. Revisiting old temptations.

"I've been through Oklahoma on a train," he said. "Grim place."

Everything was a reference to himself, she noted, without taking offence. "It truly can be," she said. "What kind of books do you write?"

"Travel books."

That struck her as funny but she'd better not laugh. She looked up. "No sign of him tonight," she said. "No sign of the lights, I mean."

"Every night, you check? And your faith is rewarded?"

"Well, faith, if you want to call it that."

"I'd call it some kind of faith."

"Maybe that's what religion is, after all—a set of habits. Turning some kind of powerful urge into a set of habits. Is it institutions, or human nature, that does that?"

By now they were taking steps back to the apartment building. He didn't answer right away. Finally he said, "Religion doesn't interest me."

He took off his glasses and rubbed his eyes. She perceived a rebuff, a rejection, and within herself, a pleasant carelessness.

"What does interest you about Alaska?" she said.

"For one thing, the food. I've never had so much good fish in my life. Every night." He turned to her with enthusiasm and replaced his glasses.

"Oh, me too!"

"The halibut is even, I don't know, sweet. It's sweet. And in two days I've had salmon cooked four different ways." Their voices rose.

"I never eat meat, so this is heaven to me," Leslie said.

"*Moi aussi*, after years of eating whatever was served to me."

"In every hemisphere."

He liked being quoted; she felt it. His lips twitched.

"Do Alaskans realize how good they have it?" Leslie went on.

"Hard to say. I haven't figured that one out. Why should they be any different?"

"Will you talk about food in your guidebook?"

"I don't write guidebooks. I didn't say that." She had offended him. But he went on after a minute. "Food, yes. I usually have something to say about food. A book won't come out of this trip, though. I'd have to come back another time. You ask a lot of questions. I'm supposed to be asking the questions."

They had arrived at their driveway.

"Time for one phone call before bed," he said at last.

"Where would you call at this hour?" Leslie asked. There was a bit of intrigue—or duplicity—in his eyes and manner that didn't go with his well-costumed exterior. He liked being asked questions.

"Hawaii. She's expecting me."

So you have love in your life, Leslie thought.

"Pleasant dreams," she said.

"And to you."

She had started up the stairs when he called out. She looked back.

"What will happen when the oil runs out?" he asked.

She paused. Was he fishing for quotes for a book?

"I don't predict the future," she said. "I try to observe the present. Long before the oil runs out, dependence has set in. That's what interests me. How does the local economy function, under the burden of this dependency? With or without royalties, it is a dependency."

"But in your previous experience, what happens?"

She looked down at him, her hand on the rail, and wanted very much to answer the question, to speculate. She perceived with a slight nausea the danger of the position he had cast her in. He was flattering her. She had said, "I don't answer questions like that," and he promptly asked her again. If she replied now, she was agreeing to the rules. It was a game. A familiar game.

"Like you said about religion," she said. "Maybe if I added predictions to my work, I'd pick up some readers. But it doesn't interest me. The minute oil is out of the ground, the minute it's targeted by some company or other, dependency sets in. That gives me plenty to think about." She looked away from him and thought for a minute. "Some economists create models to help predict the future. Models are important. Sure, someone's got to look to the future. But, not me."

He didn't have a comeback.

But he was a good-looking man, and it had been a long time since a handsome man had stood before her, below her really, in that position. A supplicant. That one weightless moment before a decision was made, and the rules of the game were thrown into place, made her feel alive.

When she thought to look for him a day later, and knocked on his door, he was gone. The guest lecturer, the visiting writer, he hadn't planned to be here long.

She looked up at green creatures in the night sky, and thought, have I turned away from one gap in my life just to concentrate on another? From my partnerless existence to this void of sky. Will he be there, won't he? Why have I settled for this, for atmospheric phenomena? Why not go farther. What about...space? The atmosphere is just the breathing jacket of the earth, after all, an extension of the planet itself. Why not leave it all behind; what else is out there? Beyond earth, beyond the pretty porch curtain of the aurora?

A week later she marked the time of the promised meteor shower on her calendar.

That night she took a warm bath, filled a thermos with hot tea, and breathed deeply with her back against the wall. Inhale through the nose. Exhale in a long, slow push of air, lips pursed like a blowhole. She rubbed her body with wheat germ–vitamin E lotion and lay down on the bed. Her life without furniture still pleased her. This bed was great. And she had learned to use the walls for back support, even for tenderness—pressing her forehead into the plaster whenever tears came.

Turned my back on one gap in my life, she thought sleepily, by turning voluntarily to another.

Finally, about midnight, she dropped off, and when the alarm rang at two she woke easily. She drank half a cup of tea from the thermos at her bedside and pulled on her clothes. Two neck warmers, snowpants, and parka. She took her flashlight into a mittened grip and stepped outside.

A light sprinkling of dry snow lay on the wooden steps going down to the street. Could it be snowing? In this bitter cold? Yes, a rare, light snow in the air. The sky was bundled in clouds. A dim, cottony ceiling covered everything. She walked up the street wide awake now, immensely disappointed and yet a bit pleased with herself, after all. She could see something of the moon through the clouds, and the street lamps glowed. No other watchers. Where was people's curiosity? But this thick, dull sky—she hadn't even considered the possibility of clouds!

A bounding presence loomed in front of her, a muscled creature shoved her leg. She leaped and cried out. It was only Chola, on the loose. They had broken the rules! The dog was out, roaming, free, neglected. She scratched its head.

"Good girl. Chola is a good girl. Come with me. But heel. Heel."

She walked on. Past the street lamps, along the ridge toward the science buildings that guarded the campus and claimed the best views, a half dozen science buildings like Rubik's cubes. One had a blue satellite dish aimed obliquely at the heavens collecting data even now. Frantic for data. She had never walked so far on her aurora expeditions. She was a little nervous, but the night was so still. The blue dish, as she watched, turned a little, adjusted itself ever so slightly. There was someone in the building. Maybe a dozen astrophysicists in there right now. Clouds no obstacle for them. I can't see the meteor shower, but there is one or there isn't; they would know, with that big old ear thing at their disposal.

She walked past the science buildings and entered the groomed swath that led through the forest to a network of cross-country ski trails. She passed another, smaller concrete cube with a circle lifted to the sky like a plate upright in a dishwasher. Then trees, and more silence. She took a ski trail down toward her right. The first kilometer was lit, so that people could ski after work. She walked on, down into the woods.

Not far, then I'm going home, she said to herself. Even unlit, the trail beyond the last lamppost glowed with a faint radiance. She wondered what nocturnal animals might be out. Wolverines, lynx, bats? But not on campus, surely.

Moose...do they sleep at night?

"Do it," she said aloud, and kept walking. It was so pretty, so filled somehow with living presence, silent watchers. The trail was wide as an alley, the snow all packed down for skate-skiers. They needed a path at least five or six feet wide. Maybe I'll go as far as the pond, she thought, at the bottom of this long, gentle slope. She had walked there in the fall and had seen the most amazing neon-blue damselflies, creatures from prehistoric times. Her boots, crudging on the dry, packed snow, and Chola's panting were the only sounds.

She did not know the temperature tonight. In her eagerness she had forgotten to check. She thought of that Jack London story about the fellow who set out without knowing the temperature in the Klondike. It came down to one chance to build a fire, one only. Look what happened to him. She laughed to herself, but still something inside of her was beginning to contract against the cold and the dark and the emptiness. She stopped walking and felt herself cringe slightly as she stared at the great, silent land.

What was that sound? She took a few steps, stopped again. A faint call, but growing louder—a howl! Leslie backed toward the trees, staring up. A moan above her, a banshee sound, something meeting death or chasing death. Her heart grew huge, pressed against her bones and skin. A geometric blackness filled the trees above her and the long moan passed right overhead.

An owl. Jiminy, that's all. Thank God. As fear left her she ached. Owls didn't attack humans, of course, but she was still shaky. Fear had tarnished her. She did not have to go as far as the lake, after all. You're not ready, she told herself gently.

Leslie started back up the trail. She heard the snow creak. It was creaking in front of her. These were not footsteps, this was like an earthquake. She stopped again. The sound now was like a daydreaming giant, taking huge, heavy purposeless steps in her direction. It was terribly loud. Leslie felt paralyzed. Which direction to move? What could it be?

Chola growled.

It was coming toward her. Leslie sidestepped off the trail into a spruce tree. Branches spilled snow onto her face. She heard the thing out there on the path, where the snow was compact. The ground shook. The air was breaking apart. Chola barked, again and again, shattering Leslie's gulps of air.

The huge shape of a moose appeared on the trail above her. Chola leaped frantically back onto the trail, barking. The moose moved steadily down the trail then stopped and stared at the frantic dog. Leslie stared at its weightlifters' shoulders. She held herself as still as ice, terrified, but the dog danced around the animal, even charging. Keeping up its deafening noise.

"Chola, no! Come!" Leslie commanded in what she hoped was a low, controlled voice. "Come here."

Chola ignored her. The moose swung its head at the dog. To Leslie's horror it raised a front leg as if to kick out at the dog. Chola barked and danced, then backed toward Leslie, barking the whole time as if bringing Leslie a trophy.

"Chola!" she shouted now. "Quiet! Quiet!"

The moose swung its head toward Leslie, then back to the dog. The dog and the moose squared off. The benign aspects of the moose were gone. It was a ton of muscle and steam and hoof, and that dog was drawing it right toward Leslie.

"CHOLA, BE QUIET."

The moose looked at Leslie.

"CHOLA!"

The dog bounded into the deep snow, toward Leslie. She tried to get hold of its collar. She could crush it into the snow, bury its head in the snow, get it to shut up. The moose stepped toward them both with its head lowered. Chola barked, as frantic, as aggressive, as ever.

"Oh please," said Leslie. "Please." She was affixed to the dog now, her hands wound through its collar. She looked at the moose then at the dog.

"CHOLA, SHUT UP!" she roared with all the seismic fury at her disposal. "SHUT UP!" On her knees she wrestled the dog off its legs. Then amazingly, it was quiet. Chola obeyed. The moose stared at them both. A long moment passed. It was as if the moose could see that the dog was a problem for them both. A concession was made. The huge animal turned as slowly as a huge ship in a small harbor, and moved off down the trail, slow step by slow step.

Leslie on her knees held Chola by the collar and the shoulders, the dog's muzzle trapped under her arm. She let her head fall onto the dog's back. She felt close to shock. But exhilaration at her release came alive inside her. The snow, the dog, her awkward posture, every physical thing felt so good, so perfect.

They crept back to the trail, her hand still in Chola's collar, and ran up the ridge, Leslie bent over. She let the dog go as they ran into the pools of electric light. Past the dishes. Keep your dishes! She wanted to shout, for no good reason.

It was after three when they got home. She brought Chola into her apartment. She climbed into bed, pulling the quilt up, and Chola settled shamelessly next to her. The dog's weight pulled the quilt tight over Leslie's body.

When she woke in the morning the black muzzle was inches from her face.

"Oh, Chola, your moms are going to be worried. And no wonder, you bad dog, troublemaker, little gangster." She excavated herself from the bedclothes and pulled on the dropped clothing from the night before.

"Let's go home, you worthless mutt. What am I going to tell them? Do I have a choice? When I open my mouth the whole story's going to flood out. I yelled at their precious dog. I coulda killed you, Chola."

She knocked on the door.

Cathy, the horticulturist, was dressed for work: a crisp man's shirt tucked into blue jeans. Her eyes lit up.

"The runaway girl!" she said. "Lee, you'll never believe what this dog has been up to! Oh, Leslie, come on in. Have some coffee." One hand slapped the dog affectionately and the other drew Leslie in by the forearm.

Artwork everywhere. A plaster torso of a naked woman. An exercise bike, an electronic keyboard. Lee, the sculptor, came out of the bedroom pulling a sleeveless t-shirt over a pair of skinny stirrup pants.

"Have a cup of coffee!" she commanded. The T-shirt was stained with paint and rust. Her bare arms were thin and golden, covered with freckles, pure muscle. She beamed at Leslie and at the dog. "And Little Schoolboys," she said. "They're good for dunking. We have them every morning. Oh, Chola, they're going to throw us off campus, all because of you, you delinquent." She squatted down and pulled back the dog's ears, glaring; then she laughed and scratched its head and shoulders. Leslie thought she was beautiful.

Leslie moved forward shyly but with determination. A box of chocolate-covered shortbread cookies, Little Schoolboys, was open next to the coffeepot. One cookie, maybe two, and then I'll go, she thought happily. Survival tasted good. Dogs and sculpture and music and cookies, and beautiful long arms. The two women pulled out a chair and poured a mug of strong, freshly ground coffee. Leslie hadn't had coffee in two years. They demonstrated their breakfast routine.

"Dunk, and then bite the head off," said Cathy. "And now, really, are you all right?"

"Oh, yes, quite. Chola and I reached an understanding. But we won't do that again, will we, Chola?" She dunked and bit. She sipped the coffee. "This is delicious. I'm ready for this, I really am."

"I don't know how she got loose. I apologize," Lee said.

Leslie wiped crumbs from her mouth. Clockwork of heaven, she thought suddenly; that's it. We cartwheel between the stars and the earth, the ground and the sky. We ride the hands of the clock. That's not so bad, is it? Thank you, thank you, thank you, someone, for this life.

"I'll take one more cookie," she said. "Thank you for these. They are heavenly."

A Secret Between
the Two of Them

Dustin Soema, who lived next door, would rub his whole face with the palm of his hand when he was tired, or when people were looking at him. He wore dark shirts like a gangster or a priest—black, purple, green. And a puffy leather jacket that Stephen thought he bought so he could pretend to be a bush pilot.

Dustin liked to pretend. Sometimes when he got out of his car at night and noticed Stephen in the driveway engaged in guerilla warfare, he would put down his briefcase and pick up a stick and spend ten minutes slipping up and down the hillside with Stephen, picking off the enemy. He was good at it. Even dying. They'd lie on the hillside ten or fifteen feet apart, legs and arms at crazy angles, dead together, shot through the heart.

Stephen would always get up first. Dustin would always wait for Stephen to resume the fight. Once Stephen saw that Dustin's eyes were closed and his mouth had fallen open; he really looked like he was sleeping.

Dustin would even play war and die when there was snow on the ground—not deep fresh snow, but the early snow in October, or the hardpack in March or April. Stephen preferred war to sledding. Always. Even when he was a little kid, and especially now that he was in fifth grade and could really roam around through the trees behind the house.

He reached the top of the power cut between his house and Dustin's and looked down the steep road to where it turned right, underneath the bent trees knocked over the road in hoops by last fall's early snow. The trees never would stand upright again. Coming up the road under those bent trees, his dad said, was like driving through a mile-long car wash. They still had their leaves on them when the blizzard came in September. The leaves took all that weight and the trees just bent right over, onto each other, onto the power lines. The houses on Stephen's road were without power and heat for a week. That was harsh, his mother said later, but they all lay in sleeping bags in the living room and read out loud and ate peanut butter sandwiches and store-bought cookies, and Stephen had not minded at all.

This afternoon Stephen was looking for Dustin's blue Trooper. February afternoons were cold, but light. The sun wasn't going down early. It was much better than December. He could stay outside longer, especially when his parents were fighting.

Stephen had draped himself with firearms—a mop handle slung over his shoulder with yarn and a Gatling gun made of pieces of Brio track, held together with duct tape. He had two empty squirt guns in his belt and a plastic knife in his boot. His mother found the knife once when they were beachcombing on a vacation. But she didn't like gun noises.

He'd be leaping around the living room, and suddenly she'd yell, "No more gun noises! That's it for tonight!"

Now the parents were inside, fighting, and Stephen had the afternoon to himself. Once a telephone came off the wall during a fight—off the wall in his mother's hands, and she threw it. It made a hole in the dining room sheetrock. Next to Stephen's chair in fact. So sometimes, especially when he was eating alone, he couldn't resist putting his fingers into the pit in the sheetrock and playing with the frayed plaster. Breaking off a little more of it. He wasn't in the room when she threw the phone, and he couldn't remember that fight, but there was the hole. There were others, too.

Stephen's mother's hands could be very nice. He liked it when she smoothed his hair and tucked him in at night. She cut the chicken off the bone for him, and cut away the skin and cut the meat. He liked chicken okay but he hated all the body parts and she cut those away.

He didn't like it when her fingers tightened on his shoulders, or when she grabbed things off the floor and said, "When are you going to pick up after yourself? Am I your servant?" The edge that came into her voice.

That edge turned her into a stranger. He wanted her to go away then. Or to go away himself. His father screamed that way too, like a blade. Stephen felt sliced. Once Stephen packed a suitcase. He packed furiously to run away. His father and mother stopped fighting and watched him.

Stephen liked it at night when his father lay down on the bed next to him and told him things and sometimes fell asleep next to him. His father would talk to him for an hour, sometimes. He'd lie down on the bed and forget what time it was and they'd talk.

Now they were fighting about something that they said had nothing to do with Stephen. Stephen sat down at the top of the driveway on the hard berm of snow. He hated it, all the screaming, the sharp edges like something broken. Stephen's left fist drilled into the hard snow beside him. The cold hurt, but it felt good too. He didn't know what to do. Sometimes there was nowhere to go. It would be nice if Dustin came home.

He waited a long time. It was almost March, and the snow was filled with things, leaves and dirt and twigs and seed things. When spring really got here a river of melting snow would pour down the side of the road. In the sunlight, water'd rush and swirl around obstacles. That was great! Every afternoon it would be different, wilder. Once it took out a neighbor's whole driveway, almost. You could put boats on it, and chase them down to the intersection and watch them come out of the noisy culvert on the other side. Water would take those boats away. You had to play in it every day, because it only lasted a week.

Stephen wondered if he could hurry things up. What if he dug a gully across the road now, into this ditch? Poured some hot water into the ditch. No, scratch that, that was silly. Once he would have done that. What he could do now, though, was move lots of snow into the ditch where the river would start. That way, it would be bigger and deeper, from the very beginning. He'd pile lots of snow at the source.

He'd have to go back to the house and get a shovel. That was okay. Stephen set down his weapons and ran down the driveway. A snow shovel leaned against the retaining wall. Not the best shovel for this job, but to get a sharper one he'd have to go inside the garage. He carried the snow shovel back up the driveway and tried to figure out where the river would start. He lived at the cul de sac on the top of the hill, so it would start around here, for sure.

Moving the snow was harder than he thought. It didn't fill the shovel easily. It didn't float on and off, the way fresh snow did in the fall, when his dad paid him to help clean the driveway. When they worked an hour or so together and then his mom came out laughing and said they were both so ripe she couldn't get within two feet of them. They wore headlamps, and they'd be out there together, warm and sweaty in the night. When Stephen wanted to stop and play soldiers instead his dad didn't mind.

Stephen tried to chisel hard snow off the bank into the ditch. He slammed the shovel blade against the snow, over and over. It was stupid. He was stupid. He walked back to the driveway and tried to stand the shovel up in the snow but it slipped away and bounced and slid down the driveway away from him.

He raised his Gatling gun and fired in a circle, 360 degrees, again and again, till enemy bullets hit him and he crumbled.

Lying still, Stephen heard a car coming up the road. He sat up and saw the dark blue nose of Dustin Soema's Trooper, coming around the curve under the birch trees. Stephen sat and watched. Dustin saw him and raised a hand just as he slowed to turn down his own driveway.

Stephen jumped up and ran down the power cut and across to Dustin's garage.

"Hello, Stephen!" said Dustin, climbing out. "What are you up to?"

"Hello," said Stephen shyly. He and Dustin never really talked much. It was funny that Dustin lived alone, but it also seemed nice, sometimes. He was wearing his bush pilot jacket today. His hair was very thick and wavy, and white on the sides. In the middle it was black, but on the sides it looked like steam coming out of a kettle. White and soft and thick.

"Been outside long?" he asked.

"Oh, I don't know," said Stephen, looking back at his house briefly.

"It's nice and light in the evening," said Dustin. "I like that. Spring is coming."

"Last year there was this big river of melted snow along the road," Stephen said. "Remember that? I want that to happen again."

"I do, indeed, it made a terrific sound."

Stephen looked back again at his own house, just to see what it looked like from here. From someone else's yard it was just another house. He wiped his nose with his free hand. He felt a little cold, from sweating so much with the shovel.

Dustin looked in the same direction.

"Your mom home today?" he said.

"My mom and dad are both home," said Stephen.

"Mm."

They stood for a few minutes in the driveway. Then Dustin said, "Do you think it would be okay if you had a glass of lemonade or something with me, Stephen?"

"Yes, I guess so. Can I help you carry something?"

"Well, yes, if you carry this briefcase, I'll get the groceries and unlock the door. Here we are."

Stephen followed him into a cool, dark kitchen. Dustin set down his bag and took off his coat. He draped the coat on the back of a chair and turned on the kitchen light. There was a table in the middle of the kitchen, and a big window over the sink. It was all very clean. Dustin pulled out a chair and told Stephen to set down the briefcase on the table. He unbuttoned his cuffs and pushed his shirtsleeves up to his elbows and rubbed his palm over his face.

"Well, Stephen," he said, "have you been to my house before?"

"I don't think so."

"Why don't you call up your folks and tell them you're here. Is that a good idea?"

"Oh, I don't have to, they don't mind. I don't have to do that, just to be at your house for a little while."

"Well, maybe we'll have the lemonade first. If we can find any." He swung wide the refrigerator door, and he and Stephen peered inside. He didn't seem to mind the cold air getting out, the way Stephen's mom and dad did. They looked together for a while till Stephen pointed to a six-pack of Minute Maid lemonade in bottles.

"Is that it?"

"There we are." Dustin took two bottles, shook them hard, and handed one to Stephen.

They unscrewed the tops and took long gulps. It was very cold and good. "Mmm," said Stephen. "Wow. I haven't had this kind before."

"Good?"

"I must be thirsty."

"You've been playing outside awhile."

"Yeah."

Dustin sat down at the table. "Sit down if you like, Stephen," he said. He opened the briefcase and took out a few pieces of mail, thin, blue envelopes. "There's a letter here from a friend of mine," he said. "All the way from Ethiopia. I wonder what he has to tell me. Shall I open it?"

"Okay."

Dustin reached behind himself, slid open a drawer, and took out a long, flat wooden knife with a carved mask for a handle. He put the blade under the flap of the envelope and slit it open. Stephen was amazed. He picked up the letter opener and rubbed the blade against his thumb while Dustin read the letter. The letter crinkled like lettuce.

It didn't make Dustin happy. He set it down and put his hand to his face again and rubbed vigorously.

"What's wrong?" said Stephen.

"My friend is telling me about my parents. I miss them, very much. The news is not bad, but they are getting old. It's a long time since I've seen them."

"Why don't you go see them?"

"Well, I can't." He picked up his lemonade and drank all of it, in two or three swallows. Then he said, "Ethiopia is not a free country, like this one. If you disagree with the government leaders, it's dangerous for you to travel there; they might arrest you and question you. I disagreed with the government once. I didn't think at the time how much I might miss my parents, someday. It's kind of surprising, really."

He smiled at Stephen and moved the envelope toward him.

"Do you like stamps? Have you seen one like this before?"

The stamp was big and showed a crowd of people waving their arms in the air. It said, "TEWODROS."

"Tewodros was a king in Ethiopia, a long time ago," said Dustin.

Stephen nodded politely and kept rubbing the knife blade. The stamp was pretty, but he didn't know what to say.

"Are you hungry?" Dustin asked.

"Yes, oh yes, a little bit."

Dustin stood up and took food out of the grocery bag—a clear plastic box of salad, a round loaf of bread, and fish in a blue foam tray.

Fish—Stephen's least favorite food. But he would have to be polite now. This was different from one of their usual afternoons together. Dustin's face looked heavy, and under his eyes the creases were deep and black.

Dustin turned toward the kitchen counter. He put a frying pan on the stove and some flour in a plate and he slapped the fish onto the plate, into the flour. He took some butter in a tub out of the refrigerator and put it in front of Stephen.

"Do you like bread and butter?" he asked.

"It's my favorite," said Stephen, happily. Dustin smiled, and his face, like a crumpled jacket, made Stephen feel good inside. Not good, exactly, something different. Not alone.

"Here's what you do," said Dustin. He picked up the loaf of bread and ripped off a chunk. He buttered it and took a bite.

"Ah," he said and handed the loaf to Stephen. "Go ahead. Rip away."

Stephen set down the knife, put his fingers into the bread, and pulled off a round piece of the heel. He put lots of butter on it. It was delicious. They grinned at each other.

"Why don't you sneak back to Ethiopia?" Stephen asked. "You could sneak in, over the border, at night, maybe crawl under the wire. Or go through the mountains."

"That's a possibility," said Dustin. "I wonder if I'm too old for that," he added, looking into space as if trying to imagine the adventure.

"That's what I would do," said Stephen. He knew that his parents would be glad to see him if he crossed an armed frontier, stealthy, fearless, quiet, in disguise. Like Tintin, or Sean Connery. His mother would cry with happiness. His father would smile and pat her and say, "Ssh, now, ssh, ssh."

The fish didn't smell too bad, sizzling in the frying pan. Dustin sprinkled something on it from a green paper can. He took two plates out of the cupboard, opened the box of salad, and dumped equal portions on both plates.

"This is called Caesar salad," he said. "Do you like it?"

"I've never had it."

"Well, do you like spaghetti? This salad is a lot like spaghetti. Very tasty. There's lots of parmesan cheese on it."

Stephen took a bite. He was astonished. He wanted another bite right away. Something about this was very, very good. It was just what he wanted, in fact.

The fish was okay too. It didn't have a strong taste at all, and it was crisp and salty. Dustin got him another lemonade. They ate all the salad and fish and a lot of the bread. It was like those times when Stephen forgot to eat lunch, and he would get so hungry he'd make a sandwich out of bread and ketchup and it would be just right.

Dustin leaned back in his chair, watching Stephen.

"You know," he said, "I don't usually tell people that I can't go back to Ethiopia. Someday things will change. The bad government will lose power, and I will go back. It is very beautiful there, in the mountains. Mostly I miss my parents, but I also miss the country sometimes. Of course, it is beautiful here in Alaska, too. And I have good neighbors."

Stephen nodded politely. He was beginning to miss his own parents.

"Should I clear the table?" he asked.

"Thank you."

"Did you do something wrong, I mean against the law?"

"I beg your pardon?"

"That you can't go back."

"There are some bad laws in Ethiopia. I may have broken those by writing an article against the government, during an election. In America, during elections, people argue a lot and that's all right. They don't expect others to think the same, even when they try to get people to agree with them."

"Well, they kind of do."

"They do?"

"My mom and dad, they get mad at each other when they don't think the same."

"Oh yes. Sure."

"I wish they thought the same, so that they wouldn't get mad at each other."

"But they don't."

"I guess they agree on the president and stuff. But they don't agree on each other. I wish they could agree on things more."

"Ah."

They sat together for a few minutes.

"Is it a secret?" Stephen asked.

"What?"

"That you wrote stories against the government, and you can't go back?"

Dustin looked thoughtful. He rubbed his face a little. "Yes, I think it is a bit of a secret. There are some people back home who don't know where I am, and maybe that's okay with me."

"I won't tell."

"Thank you, Stephen."

"I have to go now. Here, I'll take this." Stephen picked up Dustin's plate and carried it to the sink. He stacked it neatly on his own.

"Thank you for the nice dinner and all," he said.

"Thank you, Stephen."

"Bye," Stephen said. It seemed like he ought to say something else, but he couldn't think what. He picked up his mop handle.

Dustin made his fingers into a gun, pointed at Stephen, and made a soft gun noise with his mouth. "See you again," he said.

Stephen raced across the power cut, mowing down invaders. They were no match for the new, improved Stephen. He saw the snow shovel halfway up his driveway, where it had skidded into the bank, and ran up to get it. He leaped down the driveway in giant steps so that he could skid a few feet on the soles of his boots. Bullets sprayed around him. His cheeks puffed out like a trumpeter's with gun noises. Since it probably would be no-more-gun-noises time once he got inside, he'd better do it now. Loud and fast and all around the house till his parents noticed him through the glass dining room doors and called him in.

Pieta

Monty thought about leaving Kim. Almost every day he thought about it. Up here on the roof of the post office this windy September afternoon, he knew in his heart, in his gut or whatever, this was no way to live, this silent, sick, grim existence. There had to be something better. There had to be a better way than this to deal with Rinna's death. Even after the unimaginable, there had to be good times again.

Rolls of Grace roofing fabric sat about at strategic points on the vast, flat roof. Monty and Tom unrolled, measured, cut, and stapled. A job that could be so dull and hot and horrible at times was just what the doctor ordered today—methodical, rhythmic, soothing as a waltz at the Nine Mile Bar where he used to take Kim dancing. Tom Clare was a good guy to work with, quiet like a monk, always.

Heart-shaped aspen and birch leaves, the color of pure gold, lay everywhere on the black fabric. Thin and sharp, like they were shaved off of something bigger. They even covered the toes of Monty's boots. Every so often a shower of leaves would come over from the trees to the east of the building. Monty and Tom would stop and look. Then go back to work.

This afternoon's work was so pleasant, or at least pain-free, that Monty did not want to flash back to last year. Did not want to let that happen again. Tried to stop his own thoughts when he felt the memories welling up. He missed a stroke and cursed. Tom looked over; Monty waved and shook his head.

At the far end of Kim and Monty Feller's yard, the rising slough made a pleasant rushing noise against the cutbank. Normally low and silent, like tea left in a cup, for a few weeks last fall water became deeper and audible. Monty and his son Jeremiah, from his first marriage, came up the slough from the Tanana River. Kim and Monty's three-year-old, Corinna, was poised on the bank to greet them. "Get back, honey!" he called. Where was Kim?

But then Kim was right there before he even finished the thought, her arm scooped around Corinna, hauling her back.

They drew an imaginary line across the grass, three feet back from the slough. They talked and talked about it.

"Stay behind that line, Honey."

"What color is the line, Daddy?"

"It's orange. It's International Orange—no it's red, and it says: STOP."

The weather was great last fall. Kim and the kids were outside every minute. She even read the junk mail outside. She'd take out all those catalogs she got, and the laundry, and pin the laundry up, and then she'd stick her head into those catalogs and do a little bit of daydreaming about things to buy for the new house, while Corinna and the neighborhood kids played.

—

"Miz Feller, where's Rinna?"

Max, from down the road, was five years old. Kim smiled at him before answering, smiled happily at the excitement and urgency in his face.

"Well, she's here, Max. Where'd she go? Are you hiding from each other?"

"No, I can't find her. We're riding the big wheels and she went behind the rope."

"Then she's behind those sheets is all," Kim said, turning her head to look at the clothesline.

"No, dother rope, the red rope there." He pointed at the empty lawn that fronted the slough.

Slow motion, and then the speed of light. Kim turned her head and looked, slowly. Then she was over the lawn to the slough without even taking a step, she was just there, she was everywhere: no Corinna. She ran up and down the bank, she ran through the house, she kept wanting to stop and throw up, her stomach wanted to throw out this fact, fact of taking her eyes off Corinna, fact. Throw it out. Everywhere, calling.

The state troopers arrived, the neighbors, Kim looked at her watch: two hours! Two hours with no Corinna!

With every person who arrived, every phone call, Kim expected to see a grin of relief cover every face, a blonde head pop up in a car window. Over and over that failed to happen; over and over the same story from Max: "We were racing the big wheels down the ropes. Then I turn that way and she turn that way and then I can't find her. I waited for her. I can't find her. I went to ask Miz Feller where she is."

She had to describe what Corinna was wearing. What difference did it make, just rescue any kid you find in the slough, who cares what she's wearing! But she had to tell them: black rubber breakup boots with a red line along the sole, blue jeans . . . a blue sweatshirt, rhinestone earrings. She has pierced ears, like Mom.

Oh, in the days that followed, the weeks, her arms became so hungry to be filled with that familiar body, the weight just right, the softness, the life. Give me that one moment, give me back that moment. Someone put a poem in her hands, about God loaning us a sweet child. Kim stared at it in disbelief. What is this all about? She looked over at Monty who was staring at her with some kind of hope in his face, like maybe he thought this poem would help. Why couldn't he have been here that afternoon? How could Monty be thinking about anything else right now but Corinna gone? What the hell is there to have hope about?

During the funeral mass she couldn't hold her head up. She looked down at her own body. Empty arms, empty lap, flat and bereft. Every cell in her body held Corinna's absence. Every cell in her body used up, wrung out, abandoned.

Three weeks later Jeremiah turned nine. She heard Monty and his grandmother planning the party, and Kim said, "I'll make the cake! I'll make that tunnel of fudge cake he liked so much. Go on now, do something else, I'm doing this. I know what he likes."

She fought with herself to give Jeremiah his own day. She took a little pride in this show; no one else thought she could do it, but she did. The next day, she could not get out of bed. She lay there all day, studying the lack of pity in the world.

Here was a world without Corinna's small hands touching her mother's face. Mothers are big, soft dolls to small children. Corinna's arms around her neck, Corinna's hand patting her cheek, playing with her hair.

Kim stared at the space in the world that was now endless, infinite, important: space empty of Corinna. She stared.

"Sometimes I feel like leaving her," Monty Feller blurted to Tom, when their stapling brought them within three feet of each other. He hadn't planned to say a word. He didn't even introduce the subject, he just spat it out. But Tom had that way about him, he looked like someone who thought things over.

Tom could flare up, he could be a moody SOB but most often he knew how to listen. The guy was available. Though Monty had never confided in anyone about Kim and her craziness, and especially the way it wore him down, something about Tom's receptive presence next to him brought the words out. Made him erupt. As if maybe Tom could take away some of this pain.

Then he didn't want to stop talking.

But after awhile Tom said the wrong thing. He said, "My mother was never the same after my brother disappeared."

How dare he bring that up? Monty knew the story: Tom's brother, mentally ill, never showed up in town after a cross-country hike from Circle to Fairbanks, ten years ago. Yeah, Monty thought, but he was full-grown, and mentally ill besides, and he did it to himself. That's not the same.

"Even so," Tom went on, "my mom was a lot older than Kim. She had been a mother for a long time, already suffered a lot of disappointments. Had some experience of the world. They say a year isn't much, isn't enough time to know what to do next. That's what they told us."

"She's off the wall," Monty said. "Everything comes back to her grief."

"She on anything?"

"Valium. I hate it. On good days she works with this lady who makes candles and soap at home, one of those cottage industries. I hate the stuff. She always smells like a perfume factory. Actually, a little like a hospital. She smells like a hospital." Or a funeral home, he thought. That faint smell in the background all the time. Oh, Christ.

He'd give anything if she smelled of firewood or gasoline or fresh salmon, like she used to.

"The girl I married," he went on, "she was so active, a cheerleader type. Always jumping around. Muscle and spirit. Now she's in her head. All the time, in her head. And I have no clue what is going on in there."

They moved on widespread legs to the edge of the roof, bending and stapling. Tom stood up then and put one hand on his lower back, stretched. He looked out at the aspen grove across the street.

"I sure do like working high," he said. "Gives me a weird mood. Really different."

Monty wondered if Tom Clare might be a bit crazy, like his own brother, the one who disappeared. What was it that made you confide in this guy? Maybe just his name. Tom Clare. Sounds like a priest.

But Monty did not like weird stuff. He did not like the way Kim kept everything inside these days, when it was Monty's own fault, the accident, thinking he could warn a little girl back from the edge of the slough! A warning, for the love of God, he warned a three-year-old! Oh please, again, he said the prayer he had said a thousand times: I hope it was fast, make it too fast a drowning even to want her mother and father, please make it so that she died right away. Right away. Thank you, Amen.

He ruined more staples and a stretch of fabric. Tom lent a hand, and when they finished the repair, still on their haunches, gasping a little, Tom put his hand on Monty's arm.

"So today you feel like leaving her," he said. "Yesterday? Tomorrow? Go ahead and say it, at least to yourself, say it every day, how it feels. Tomorrow, for instance. Tell someone."

Monty's face burned. Christ, he thought, will you shut up with your advice? What do you know? Tom didn't have a wife or a child either one. Least as far as anyone knew. Who's to know. He moved forward to the next grid of roof to be covered, swung the roll of Grace lengthwise, kicked the bulk of it so it rolled out like a carpet. Very unprofessional.

"The girl I married," he said. "I keep thinking that: Where is that girl? How can she disappear so completely? Do you know what I'm even talking about?"

"Yeah, I think." Tom walked patiently the length of the fabric, straightened it, lifted his knife from his hip.

Stuff it now, Monty thought. I'd better save my shit for another time. I need this job. Do it right.

"Truth is," said Tom, "even in good times, the people we know disappear. Because if nothing else, Monty, young people turn into older people. You just have to believe there's a girl in there who's waiting for some kind of help, some kind of something, I don't know."

It was forty miles after work to get home, down the Richardson Highway to the Fellers' road. Monty stopped off these days at the Nine Mile Bar for a cold one. Helped a little.

The girl I married, he thought. He shouldn't even go there because that was some kind of lie. That was a dead end. There is no such thing. That's what Tom was saying. The girl I married. Kim had the yellowest hair, and great legs. She played volleyball. She'd run around on the lawn and muscles would move under her skin. Made her legs change shape, and every shape, each and every one, was beautiful. And firm. God. Her torso was so small and firm, all of that and she was just so gentle. The way her fingers moved up his neck into his hair. Drove him crazy. "I'm comin' after you," that's what it meant. She loved making things nice for Jeremiah, too. She loved that house they built, filling the pantry with pickled green tomatoes, blueberry jam, canned smoked salmon. What a sight that was. She never got wired, like other women, rushing around like she was so damned important. She just did these nice things.

Now, she was broken glass inside. Or wacko on Valium. There'd be eggshells in the scrambled eggs, the salmon burned. Wild eyes looked into the next room, right past him.

He would have done anything to make her feel better. She rejected every single offer.

He could see two strange cars in the driveway, one of them oh no a State Trooper's car. Monty parked carefully and climbed out and walked toward the house. On the front porch people he didn't know looked at him and then went inside the house, leaving Kim and Jeremiah on the steps. Monty gasped with relief: his son and his wife were okay.

He hadn't even put words to his panic yet, but to see them there, staring back at him, tears came to his eyes and he thought: whatever it is, they are okay. This is relief I'm feeling. Whatever happens now, it doesn't matter compared to this I swear to God.

He walked closer. Kim had something in her lap, and between the two of them he saw what looked like an old plastic tricycle. A big wheel. Was it Corinna's?

"Dad," called Jeremiah.

"Hey," said Monty, and he held out his arms.

Jeremiah's face was puffy. He had been crying. Monty grunted and hoisted him, and the boy's legs wrapped around his father's hips. Monty walked up on the porch, over to Kim. She looked different. Her left hand lay on the handlebar of the big wheel, her right arm cradled something in her lap. Her eyes, shining with tears, looked directly at him, right at Monty, right into his heart.

"They found these about a half mile down," she said softly.

She hadn't looked at him like that for the whole year. She had not wanted to look at him at all.

Monty looked down at her lap. A boot, a child's black rubber boot with a red line around the sole. Corinna's. They'd found it, then. It was twisted, pinched at the ankle.

"It was wedged in the trike. Who knows when or how that happened. She couldn't stop herself, or maybe it happened in the water."

Monty sat down in the empty chair next to Kim's. Corinna's last journey. The river took her, he thought in wonder. He put his hand on Kim's arm. He waited a long time. He let his eyes rest, looking out over the golden tops of the trees, resting in the far distance, in the empty sky. He didn't realize until that moment that he had been straining every day to see her again, to see her waving confidently from the safety of her own home, waiting to see her restored to her mother's eyes.

Hawks Over Water

Early afternoon on a sunny March day in 1999 in Fairbanks, in a coffeehouse near the university, two women sat sidesaddle to the table between them. The blonde, tall and leggy, in her mid-forties, wore black jeans and a long green sweater. Strands of glinting hair rose up from her head with static as she leaned on her elbows, chin on her hands. Her companion was plumper, younger—barely tamed black and gray curls fanned out around her heart-shaped face. She had spent the morning in a classroom, leading a discussion of post–World War II feminist literature in Germany.

The blonde was between jobs, an aspiring writer. She had slept late, picked the jeans up off the floor where she had dropped them the night before, ripped the green sweater off a hanger in her crowded closet with a gesture that spilled more hangers and dresses to the closet floor. But she had made her appointment on time. She always did that, hearing her mother's voice in her mind: "Punctuality is a matter of how you were raised."

A mug of maté tea, a plastic tumbler of iced granita, a napkin with crumbs on it, and a thick manuscript inside a three-ring binder—the purpose of their meeting—filled the space between them. Melina Leader, the blonde woman, was preparing to offer her mother's journal to the university press: the daily life of a woman in northern Michigan—thirty years of running a backwoods lakeside resort, raising five children alone.

Aqua-blue sticky notes flared from the top and sides of the manuscript like lettuce leaves sticking out from a sandwich. Tori Tarbell, the professor of comparative literature, had just finished reading it and the sticky notes were hers—comments, suggestions, copy editing. "Parts of it are funny," she said. "That's what surprised me. The humor."

"Me too," said Melina, the youngest daughter of the woman who had written the journal, Mary Leader, who had died the previous summer. She pushed the napkin here and there on the table with long thin fingers. Tori watched the gesture; she admired Melina's hands. She liked watching the way Melina held herself together against the chaos of life, even at the advanced age of forty-six, six years older than herself. Melina, in her evergreen sweater and black jeans, with her bizarre hazel eyes—one green, one yellow and green—made Tori want to hum the "Tennessee Stud." *The color of the sun and her eyes are green…*

"Because the basic facts…" Melina was saying.

"The facts are not funny."

"They're not," Melina agreed.

"Marketing angles are sticking out like ripe berries, I tell you," said Tori. "Henry David Thoreau before us as a single mom!" she chortled. "You're well off with that funny, naïve sort of angle, a little salt to cut the—well, the sadness of it, the emotion of it. Jesus. Her naïveté is a nice way into the story. Can I say that, naïve?"

"If that's what you think."

"A family discovers the real world. The solipsism of the family, the lure of the outside world. Children on their own, largely, because that is what you were, drawn again and again to the edge and then retreating back to your cluster."

"Oh, come on. She was a strong and caring presence, even when she wasn't home. I dread to think what would have happened to us if she even once had said, 'I'm not equal to this.'"

"It's not humanly possible to be both mother and father to five children."

Tori loved the sound of her own words. Melina could feel the pleasure her friend was taking, even now, in making apt pronouncements. She listened to the high notes of discovery in Tori's voice as if to a familiar piece of music. This was the sound of Melina's own mother's voice, hunting for the words to describe a particular view or plant or animal in northern Michigan. Her thrill as she discovered order in the universe: the thrill of reading the codes correctly, of finding oneself to be the code breaker and announcing her find.

She thought, watching Tori's animated face, I'm addicted to this, the vigorous expression of an opinion. This is my Mozart. But my mom had something else, too—an ability to listen—no, a compulsion to listen. She kept her ear to the ground, had genuine curiosity.

On the whole, it's quite a positive story. But some of it is so sad. That just one death, my father's death in August 1955, had such lasting effect—went so deep and changed everything.

Friday, September 23, 1955. The autumnal equinox; twelve hours of light, twelve of dark. A squall threatened in the afternoon, but the rain didn't come. Instead, while the temperatures were mild, the wind picked up; it drove over the surface of Achill Lake, beat against the shoreline resorts and cottages, roared in the cedars.

Mary Leader walked out onto the dock at Pinestead Resort, far enough out to where she felt the power of the wind-whipped lake around her. The wind's battering held her upright, reminded her that she was still alive. Turquoise lake water threw itself up in beautiful, wild pyramids. Jim had always loved this face of the lake.

She put her hand flat on her stomach as she saw him again, in her mind's eye, as vivid and powerful as if he were standing in front of her—that grin as he looked at the rough water, checked the direction of the wind.

Mary walked farther out, to the end of the narrow, weathered cedar planks. In a day or two the dock would come apart in sections when Chris Olivet, the handyman, waded out into the water to break it down and haul it up into the boathouse to be stored for the winter.

Pinestead Resort was closed for the season. The last batch of guests left over a week ago. Normally the Leaders would be back home in Chicago by now, the older kids already in school. So it had always been before, in the several years they had owned this place. But now nothing was normal.

Mary sat down on the end of the dock. The wind was almost warm, glorious really. She thought, so many things are over now: running this little resort in upstate Michigan, windy afternoons on Achill Lake after everyone else has gone home, Indian summer and the striking colors, . . . Just the two of them, then gradually up to seven of them, five children in ten years.

Then, good-bye. No, no good-bye. Just gone.

All those quarrels—because Jim Leader did not marry a dishrag, did not marry a little helpmate—quarrels that ended only when one of them would say, "I'm leaving!" and the other would rejoin, "Fine, but take these kids with you!" That sharp retort would put a stop to all talk of leaving. Until he found a way to leave and not take the kids.

Pulmonary embolism—a silent, efficient killer, a bullet in the bloodstream.

As she sat there on the edge of the dock, the pain came back, rotated like a spiked wheel in her chest. She couldn't even sit up. She collapsed slowly onto her side against the hard planks. Hope left her like air leaves an old rubber raft deflated for winter storage. Hope and strength and tautness and resistance, she had none of these.

Mary, a nurse, stared at the water like a patient staring at an IV bag.

This time the tears that finally filled her eyes and moistened her face were tears of self-pity, pure and simple: she was so tired of the pain. After six weeks she was tired enough to lie here without the strength even to wail *leave me alone!*

But after a while she sat up again, rubbed her face dry. What the hell was she dragging it out for? Chris could handle everything. Chris would have to handle everything—shutting down the place, getting it ready for sale.

"Getting it ready for sale," she said loudly, to no one.

This too, losing this place—one thing after another. Go home to Chicago, where Grandma Leader and Jim's unmarried sister, Antonia, can help with the kids. Go home to Chicago, to their heavily mortgaged, crowded house in Wicker Park. Not much life insurance. A plastic surgeon but with no interest in cosmetic surgery, and just barely getting started. Jim wanted to repair birth defects, eager to give away his skills in craniofacial surgery. *You have a family to provide for,* she used to argue silently. Didn't think he'd die. A doctor, but didn't think he'd himself catch what it was he treated patients for, mortality. Oh not him. Life insurance? They couldn't afford it, with the mortgage and five kids!

"Damn you!" she screamed, suddenly standing up and looking behind her, at the land, at the cedars, the boathouse, the four small cabins, the five dented aluminum canoes up on shore, the big house, the motorboat in its hoist, the green swing on the bank, the three tall swallow houses on upright poles.

"Butcher!" she screamed. At whom? Go home to Chicago? "You go home to Chicago!" she screamed again. "It was never my town!"

Chris, the handyman, might hear her, but so what. He was working in the garage, on one of the outboard motors. He'd likely hear her even though it was noisy—the wind was noisy, the trees were noisy, the waves slapping at the boat and the dock, all noisy. Slap and fall of water, roar of the cedar trees, nothing more.

—

"But what will you do with all the stuff that she does *not* write about?" asked Tori. "Her depression, the way you girls were on your own so much, well and I guess her despair? She talks like she faced facts and got over it."

"She didn't."

"Well, *no*. You don't." It was out there again, that strong confident voice, Tori in her element.

Melina drank the last of her tea, folded the paper napkin into a small closed blossom, and poked it into her empty glass mug. She uncrossed her legs, stretched back in the chair, and crossed her ankles. She folded her left arm across her body, rested her right elbow on her left wrist, rested her cheek in her right hand, and stared at a poster on the wall. A jazz musician, young, beautiful, head wreathed in cigarette smoke, open white shirt, his fingers resting so delicately on the stem of his saxophone. Killing himself with drink and cigarettes. Lovely self-destruction. I'd like to go there. Have a drink and a smoke. Not care anymore. She gave the feeling a minute or two to sink in, let it encircle and inhabit her, until her stomach dropped and she actually had to draw a deep breath.

Who am I kidding, I don't have *a drink*. Never had *a drink* in my life. I have six or seven drinks. I don't have *a drink* and *a smoke*. Don't kid yourself.

Oh you kid, her mother used to say. Mary Leader didn't have *a drink* either. She had four or five beers, Drewry's, stubby brown bottles kept cool and out of sight on the cellar shelves. And sometimes gin out of the flat bottle she kept under her mattress.

Melina returned to the subject at hand—introducing and refining her mother's manuscript. Tori, a precocious scholar, had been an editor for five years; besides being a hawk-eyed critic of manuscripts, she had a sixth sense for what might sell. Melina had wondered what to say in her introductory notes: what background to give, what tone should a daughter assume?

"I love her voice just as it is," said Melina. "And I hate to come down all—all, like, all-knowing—omniscient—in an introduction. It wouldn't be fair, but worse, it would be inappropriate. Like the wrong frosting on a cake. Know what I mean?"

Tori laughed, thinking about wrong frostings. But she quickly seized on the more interesting idea, that a daughter's life and a mother's life could be such different stories, there's no way they automatically fit together, or even belong in the same solar system.

"My mother still prays for me," Tori said suddenly. "After all these years, she still prays that I will see the error of my ways."

Tori had a full and vibrant face, a curvaceous body, she emanated warmth and excitement even when pontificating; but whenever she talked about her own mother, an evangelical Baptist, her face turned flat and mannish, her lips straightened. Melina envied her friend for having living parents, but she wondered, not for the first time in a friendship going back ten years, if Tori's stunted emotion when it came to her mother, her flat voice when speaking of her, came from particular pain, from injuries.

"She prays that I'll be free of Satan," Tori went on.

"I think I can believe in God," said Melina. "I really do. But Satan is a stretch." She wanted to say more, to learn more about the reality of Tori's upbringing—to understand more and then to say the right thing, the comforting thing. But as usual, Melina was too slow; Tori couldn't wait. She leaped away from the discomfort of the topic—just as she would leap back into it, time and again.

"Oh well," she said. "I was supposed to be a certain way, I let her down."

"How is Serena?" asked Melina.

"Blooming," Tori announced happily. Ardor returned to her face as she talked about her daughter, a high school senior who was an exchange student in Argentina.

To Mary Leader's surprise, screaming into the wind felt good, and two or three shouts weren't enough. She felt her energy returning with each bellow. She flung her head back to scream again and that's when she saw the first hawk.

It rode against the wind over the roof of the boathouse. Breast to the wind. Like the sail of Jim's dinghy, pressed against the wind when he would take the kids out one at a time for a ride. As she stared, she saw another, and then another. Then, to her astonishment, she counted five. She had never seen hawks pushing against the wind like this, and she had never seen hawks in a group. She stared up until her neck hurt.

Then she saw Chris on the grassy bank above her. She waved to him to come and see the birds. He held a Johnson outboard in his arms, and he looked alarmed. Heard her shouting, maybe? She waved again, a wave to say, *I'm all right, don't worry,* and another wave to say, *Come here quick and see this!*

Chris Olivet was one of those off-by-themselves bachelors, younger than her but already set in his ways, a woodsman. He liked to sculpt and paint, and to hunt deer, black bear, and ducks. All he wanted out of a job it seemed was just enough money to keep doing those things for his own satisfaction, or maybe to meet other personal compulsions, whatever they might be. He worked alone. He'd accept a cup of coffee from her in the morning, work all day by himself. Jim always told her, "Some men up here are like that," when she wondered about Chris's solitude.

"He needs a family," she would say. "He's so capable, he's nice, he's young."

"Leave him be," Jim would say.

Chris set the motor down on the grass and came out on the dock toward her. She waved toward the sky. They both looked up then as more hawks appeared over the ridgeline of the boathouse. Seven of them! Chris's knees bent suddenly as if the sight had cast a spell, enough almost to knock him down.

"I've never seen anything like that," he said. "Heard you calling, I thought something was wrong."

"Well," she said loudly over the wind, "Something is terribly wrong, of course—things couldn't be more wrong, could they?"

He gave her a quick, cautious look.

"Could they?" she said.

"No, missus, they couldn't," he said. They looked back at the hawks, which had started to rise on the wind and drift away toward the east, out of sight. They were higher in the sky now, drifting away. Mary lowered her head and rubbed her aching neck. Chris said, "I thought the world of Dr. Leader. I wish I could help more."

"Thank you," she said. Chris always wore ripped flannel shirts half-buttoned over frayed T-shirts, blue jeans spattered with paint and grease. Some of that paint was house paint, some was colorful stuff from his own easel. His face was unremarkable except for its intensity, and the acne scars. Did the scars set him aside, scare the girls away, she had wondered when she first met him. Or was it the intensity. A girlfriend would modify that intensity. "Leave him be," Jim said. "Some men are like that."

"The motor's all right now," he said. "I'll put it back in the boathouse for the winter. I'll put the boats and canoes there too. And I want to get that section of roof reshingled while it's warm."

"Send me your bill," she said, "when you're ready."

Chicago. I'll be in Chicago. Assumption Parish School again for the three oldest I suppose, the other two with Grandma and Tony maybe. And me—full time at Children's Hospital? How will I manage? Where else could I go?

"They're back," said Chris suddenly, and he pressed her forearm to get her to look up. This time it was she who nearly fell over. The seven hawks were lower, just above the boathouse. They must have turned and powered back for another ride. The dark, terrifying shapes floated almost directly above her. Her neck was flung so far back, she held onto Chris's sleeve so as not to lose her balance. The wings sliced so casually, irrevocably into the air. It seemed as though the hawks floated against the wind just because they wanted to, just because they could.

A turning of black wings. The strangeness of it made her shudder, but it was good, a wonderful feeling, the terrible consolation of it. Their bodies, from the underside, so big they could shade the sun. Big and mysterious as death.

"Never seen that before," said Chris, who had grown up in this area. A hunter, a fisherman, an artist, but he had never seen this. They stood on the dock, in the wind, almost in fear until once again the hawks drifted east, let the gusts push them east against the hill, away from the lake.

Mary shook her head in wonder.

"You never know what you might see in these woods," he said. "It's different all the time. I never get tired of it. Never."

"What's it like in the winter?"

"Last year one time the lake froze over and the snow blew off, left it clear and hard. Went out there on the ice with a couple of neighbors. Looked down six feet into that clear ice. You never saw anything like it. We was ice skating every day for a week, skated from here to Deer Meadow. Sometimes in Round Lake where it's so shallow, you see turtles swimmin' along under the ice, underneath where you're skatin'. *Where are the rich people now, I wonder,* we said to each other. Don't mean you, Mrs. Leader."

"No, Chris. I'm not rich. And I don't know what I'm going to do. This resort was just a way for us to be able to afford to come north in the summer. Get away from the city. Jim loved the woods and the lake, you know, fished every chance he got."

"Yes he did."

Chris would know; he took Jim fishing often enough. Down the Manistee, the Lebanon, the Sandy, up to the UP, all through the chain of lakes. Mary had stopped going fishing about the time of the third baby. She liked camping, but fishing struck her as boring. She liked to be outside as much as the next person, more even, but not just sitting there, waiting for a bite. Good grief. Not that. Those men out in the bass boats at dawn. How could they stand it?

But to be outside working, walking, canoeing. That was the best.

"I wonder, Chris, if my family could live here year-round."

"Missus?"

"We got this place, why should we turn our backs on it, go back to where we are really at a disadvantage in so many ways, even dependent on Grandma Leader?" Why was she talking to him like this? Mary was a private person; she didn't buttonhole people and beg their advice. Why was she staring at Chris? *Give me a green light, oh please help me,* she thought.

"I'd never be able to live in a city," he said simply.

"I live for summers up here," she said. "But maybe kids need more than what this place offers. I suppose the isolation here in the winter isn't so good for kids."

"Not good for kids? The woods?"

"They need schools."

"Schools up here, Ma'am. I went to Miltonia High School."

"Well yes, but, other things."

"I guess Dr. Leader needed to be near the big hospitals, anyway."

"Yes, that's it." And what other things, she thought, do kids need? To be just like other kids, or to see hawks over water?

In Chicago there won't be Jim anymore. Chicago is a killer wind barreling at you. Five o'clock and dark already on a winter night, and I'm sitting on a wheezing, gasping bus trying to get home to the kids from Children's.

Or, I could give my kids this.

"Chris, what does the big house need, if we stayed here all winter?"

"You and the kids?"

"Shingles, you said, and firewood maybe."

"Missus, you'll need more than firewood."

"What then?"

"There's some forced-air heating in the house, but I don't believe anyone has used it for some time. You need to overhaul that furnace, and there's places in the house where you can build up the insulation."

"Would you take a look at the furnace?" *What if we stayed here? What if my kids and I stayed, just for one winter maybe? What kind of a mother would I be, not to give them this—the wilderness—to temper our loss?*

They won't have the Art Institute and the best schools, but they could have hawks; they'd have the lake and wildlife and trees. You died, Jim, you don't get a say anymore. Serves you right. What am I supposed to do, limp ahead in the life we planned even though you aren't here? Or do something better, something different? There's so much work to do here, the place itself will help me raise these kids. The outdoors will help me. I won't have to supply all the busy work, the entertainment—nature will help me.

She looked up again. She could still see hawks to the east. A registered nurse could find some kind of work in winter around here. Seems like the best idea, if you ask me—and there's no one else to ask anymore. Who's going to stop me?

Melina's mind wandered. She mused silently that she might someday write a memoir about those early years after her father died, of those years growing up on the lake in Michigan, before she came up here to go to college. She'd expand on her mother's journal, fill in some of the details, and contemplate the meaning of those events in retrospect. She'd probe her sisters' memories, search for useful references in old copies of the weekly *Achill County News*. And she could start her story with that fateful September day all those years ago when their lives were turned irrevocably in a new direction, that day when her mother and Chris Olivet stood on a weather-worn dock, transfixed, as above them seven hawks pushed into the wind, turned, rode with the wind, drifted off, returned.... What to call it? Epiphany at Achill Lake? A Spell on the Water? Hawks Over Water?...

"That she never married again," said Tori. "Never even dated. So different from us. I feel I have a couple of romances left in me, even now!" She laughed at herself.

"No kidding," said Melina. "There was a fellow she met at the Grand Canyon, in her sixties. They were fond of each other, wrote letters for a couple of years.

"How about that handyman? Chris Olivet?"

"No, romance wasn't part of that. She didn't know him all that well. He was younger, very much a loner. But there's a story—a couple of years after we moved up to Achill Lake, after my father died—she was sitting on a barstool somewhere, and Chris gave her a talking to. He told her, 'You have to pull yourself together. You have no choice; you have to do it for those kids.' It was a real turning point for her. I heard that story, versions of it, several times. I don't know how it came about, that they were in a bar together, but that's the story. She was desperate and he laid it out. You got to do this."

"And she did."

"She did."

"But later on, he..."

"Yeah. When I was about ten. That was awful."

"Do you think she had any idea why?"

"Oh no. By that time we didn't even see him that much. He was always a loner. Nobody ever talked about a reason for his death. Her main take on that was that he should have gotten help with whatever was troubling him, and that suicides are people who give up. She said it's a sin and a waste of life, and life is precious and you don't waste it." Melina glanced around at the artwork on the walls of the coffeehouse, looking into the past. Trying to remember. To be fair. What else?

"His wasn't the only one. She didn't have a lot of sympathy for suicides. Let me put that a different way." Melina thought for a minute. "She would be angry, taking care of an attempted suicide. She'd be impatient and angry in a way you wouldn't expect from a nurse. Judgmental, is that the word?"

"Even though this was the man who once talked her out of despair."

"They handled things differently in those days, that's for sure." She studied her friend across the table, grateful for Tori's interest. It meant a great deal to Melina that Tori found the manuscript between them worth this trouble. And Melina felt oddly relieved to have this chance to talk about her mother. This is my bargain with death, she thought. A good thing.

Tori didn't fiddle with things, or fling her arms about as she talked; her animated face was the guide to her feelings. Her salt-and-pepper curls brushed the magnificent Turkish scarf around her shoulders. She put her fingers on the loose knot of the scarf as if to remind herself that she owned such a thing. Tori liked being able to afford good clothes. She had worked hard against terrific odds to become a professor, but she still felt that her upbringing shadowed her like a wounded relative, demanding attention at inappropriate moments.

Out of nowhere, right now, she felt a mild resentment welling up toward her friend, a resentment of Melina's seemingly more protected upbringing. Sheltered on the shore of Achill Lake. Sheltered by something, what? Melina had this freshness about her that no one should still have approaching fifty. How did she come by it? How could she be so, so—what's the right word? Surely not innocent at our age. Protected, that's the right word.

Poverty, hellfire, bad taste. That was Tori's background. At least, that's what she sometimes thought, in her saddest moments.

Then she remembered the spoon.

Instantly her face lit up. She touched the curly hair against her temples, smoothed it back.

"My mom, when she moved to the new apartment, sent a few things up here," she began. "She sent some of my books, a quilt I liked, a few other things. And, when I opened the box, on top of everything, she had set this spoon. Not a valuable spoon, just happened to be the one I always chose to use, growing up. I liked to eat my cereal with it. It has a flowery silvery handle, a nice round bowl. Just my favorite spoon. I don't remember ever talking to her about it. How did she know? But she did know."

Melina smiled too, hungry for such stories and thinking about mothers and daughters. "She probably did lots of things like that, from time to time, when you were growing up. She watched you. She knew."

"Yeah, well, maybe. I don't know."

"Does she have friends, your mom?"

"No, Lord, she has the church."

They sat quietly for a few moments. Melina brushed the fan of aqua-blue sticky notes lightly with her fingertips.

The coffeehouse was filled with sunlight, some reflected off the snow outside. Students in grungy vests and pants the color of wheat or old grass, some with dreadlocks, came and went, fondled issues of local papers that were lying about, greeted each other, parted company. It seemed to Melina that the afternoon had become ripe and even peaceful. As if she and Tori had arrived, briefly, at a well-deserved intermission, pulled up their boats to sit on the sand. An afternoon in which to be glad that we have some experience, some hard-won judgment—at long last you might say—so we can look at a manuscript together and trust each other to reach for the truth.

Tori thought about her mother's deep-set, shadowed eyes. She could see those large, troubled eyes gazing at her, but sometimes—sometimes, they weren't filled with reproach and sadness, but with pleasure. Pleasure in her daughter. Sometimes when they looked at each other, there was no need to talk. She thought about how her mother must have smiled, packing that spoon. Tori had a daughter in Argentina to whom she herself sent care packages. She knew.

Fooling the Guesser

Paul escaped the party to gather more wood for the fire. To be outside, coatless, in the frigid black box of the night was a relief. He needed a break from his wife's people—especially nights when they seemed just that, his wife's people, though surely they were all his friends, too, after thirty years in Fairbanks.

Thirty years ago he'd spent a winter not far from here, squatting in a miner's cabin he'd found in the woods. Barely room to turn around inside. Walking home from school on a winter night, he might step into an abandoned mine shaft and disappear and no one would check on him for days, not even a sled dog. At twenty he found that thought intriguing. But now, Christ, he and his wife, Deena, were listed in symphony programs, their names engraved on a ceramic tile at the public library!

Paul filled his left arm with dried firewood, holding it the way he used to hold Anna and Robert, his children. Now fifteen and, thank God, only twelve, he still had one child. Still had a way to go with that one. He looked up at Orion the hunter in his December position, to the right of the woodbox, just above the hill. The Pleiades above him like groupies.

Behind him, inside the house, the party was still going strong, as strong as parties could go these days, since people no longer drank quite as much, no longer smoked. The thing he really missed was that passionate, overbearing argument that used to yield gems. Not much of that these days. He was never a talker himself, but he liked listening to his friends solve the world's problems. Nowadays caution had taken over. Half the people inside were involved in local politics, eager to build coalitions. It made them cautious. There was a state representative in there, a school board member, a guy who worked for the mayor, and the public defender. Even Deena was on the public library commission. It's made conversation hard work, Paul thought. The path of righteousness is overgrown with complications.

On the other hand, the food was better than ever. Woks full of nutritious, spicy, low-fat concoctions covered the kitchen counter along with crockery bowls filled with fruit salad or couscous. A person could eat thirds, if he wanted. Paul planned to have thirds himself, after he got the fire going again. It gave him something to do. And since he'd started going to AA two years ago his taste was keener, his pleasure in eating renewed.

He carried the wood toward the porch, his boots grinding over snow dry as sand, and he remembered suddenly, intensely, the day that he and Eliza Markey, one of the women inside, had skied down the hill behind him on just such a thin blanket of snow. Almost too little for skiing, but what a day. Deena was visiting her family in New York at the time. That was when she learned that her mother had Parkinson's. Hard times were coming. But Paul had enjoyed being alone. He soaked in the solitude every day like a man too long deprived.

Then Eliza Markey had called him about something, some political event no doubt, and they were talking and before he knew it he asked her to come skiing.

She looked radiant that day. A red wool muffler tied around her neck, she looked like a present. Glowing skin, big smile, dark hair in smooth shiny curls escaping from underneath her cap. And those wide, exotic cheekbones. Leaning on their poles, victorious after a two-mile downhill glide, they gazed at each other and he wanted to kiss her. He thought, someday.

They came inside after skiing and he made tea and turned on the radio. When a certain song came on they suddenly looked at each other, startled, overjoyed, and they each thought—he was sure of this—they wanted to dance. It would come so naturally. He remembered moving toward her with his arms lifting, and stopping himself, at one and the same moment. She stared right back at him, eagerly, he thought, but waiting. And the music changed, too soon.

He could still remember how that felt. Should he have taken her in his arms? He had never been able to answer that question. It was history now, something that happened and something that didn't happen.

There'd been times since then when he thought he would be willing to split in two, to risk his marriage, after all, but it never happened, with anyone. Twenty years of marriage. Sure, it could still go belly up. Not out of the woods yet. It happened to others all the time. Eliza Markey, she'd been married three times.

Paul crossed the porch, grasped the door latch with his right hand, shoved his boot inside and pushed the door open.

Faces looked up, smiled. Robin Rowe, the public defender, came to help him with the wood. A woman in a Pakistani shirt covered with embroidery and tiny mirrors was crossing the room with a plate of food. She held a spoonful of blueberries halfway to her mouth and stared at Paul and Robin as they knelt by the stove. She was the new professor of American literature, Molly something. Long brown hair and eyes of mixed colors, one green, one brown. Very young, and a little on the plump side. Deena said she was writing a book on Willa Cather.

Most of the people here were affiliated with the university, but not all, thank God. They weren't ghettoized that severely, not yet anyway.

Robin was head of the public defender's office, and Eliza Markey and her new husband both worked downtown. Paul, an engineer, worked at the city power plant. Deena, who taught creative writing at the university, had just published her second novel. This party was in lieu of the publication party they had been too busy all summer to have.

Paul wanted to ask Deena if she too had noticed a strange weariness in the air tonight, a lack of luster. But that wouldn't be nice: it was an important party for her, that novel had been a bear to finish. Still, listen to these conversations. Here they were, the progressive movers and shakers of Fairbanks, celebrating a new novel and yet—they were discussing movies. They were raving about the joys of subscribing to Netflix and sharing favorite titles.

Of course he finally joined in. No one liked the recent Alaska movies, *The Edge*, even though it had Alec Baldwin and Anthony Hopkins, or *Limbo* by Sayles, or *Salmonberries*. Foreign films sneaked in, and the crowd warmed up. *Zentropa, Nasty Girl, My Life as a Dog, Babette's Feast,* the fabulous new Spanish movies by Almodóvar. Molly, in the Pakistani shirt, said that she liked an old movie called *Diary of a Country Priest*. There was a short silence—was she religious? Then she started talking about a German film called *The Man Inside*. It sounded good. People wrote down the title.

Paul saw his daughter Anna studying the array of dishes in the kitchen. Her hair, rippled like Deena's, fell to her waist. She wore blue jeans and a hockey jersey and curled her stocking clad toes in anticipation as she filled her plate. What a beautiful, perfect child she was, redeeming his life, growing by inches every month almost, growing in her sleep. He had done right to keep certain things from her—certain cares—however he had managed it. She was getting the most out of being a high school girl, and he loved to see it. He would do anything to keep her from seeing too much of the world too soon.

Robin Rowe had nothing to contribute to the movie conversation. No point in mentioning his own favorite, *The Hunt for Red October*. He came back to the woodstove and took over the tending, stoking it with neat lengths of dried cottonwood. He thought: I wish there were some criminals here so I'd have someone to talk to. His wife, Kate, sensed his discomfort and smiled at him frequently from across the room. Robin was a famously shy, often red-faced man with a long, gray beard, meticulously attired tonight for the courtroom, where he had spent his day. There had been no time to change.

"I love that smell," Eliza Markey was telling her third husband, meaning the smell of wood smoke. No one else here knew it, but Robin had defended her first husband against domestic assault charges sixteen years ago, and lost, happily—the man was guilty. Eliza did not hold this against Robin or refer to it. She treated Robin with kind consideration for his obvious fish-out-of-water qualities whenever she ran into him. He had been a son of a bitch, Clyde Markey. She would have just left him, taken their two sons and left, but he wanted custody, so she went after the criminal record he deserved. Robin defended Clyde because that was Robin's job, and his job, lucky for him, contained his values. Not many men were that lucky these days. And without his values, Robin knew, a misfit like himself would be in some deep trouble indeed. Those values he could identify, he stuck with.

In court, he remembered, Eliza seemed almost like a sleepwalker. He knew, just looking at her, that she had been beaten. It interested him that she kept the name—Markey.

They had never talked about it since. No problem. There were lots of events and people Robin Rowe never talked about, not ever, with anyone but Kate.

But especially he would not talk about Eliza Markey. If he could do something for her, he would. Such feelings were mistaken, he knew. Women no longer wanted to be looked after in this world. But the feeling a woman like Eliza started inside him, the feeling of gentle solicitation, was pleasant to him. As long as he kept it to himself. No one had to know. Once at the school science fair he started to help her take down her son's exhibit. For a second he was embarrassed, thinking he had given himself away, but shortly another dad was there too, asking her where she wanted to put the wooden waterwheel, folding the poster board. That was one time she herself was between husbands. Or was it just that her husband was out of town? Was there ever a time she was between husbands, or had all these guys overlapped?

"There's a moon outside that one would not believe," said Anton, the professor of theater, as the heavy wooden door swung open again and a curl of frigid air raced across the room, hitting people's legs like a small dog. Anton pulled off his leather gloves and then his black neck warmer with a flourish. The raven-black hair on his head followed the neck warmer skyward. He smoothed it down.

Students loved Anton, so Robin heard. He had come to Fairbanks from St. Petersburg, Russia, two years ago. He seemed a wild card to Robin. Had Anton been perhaps a criminal in his native land? There was a bit of something duplicitous about him. You didn't know how far to trust him; but in the theater department, that flamboyance served him well. It was possible that Anton dyed his hair. But let's face it, Robin thought, he's a lively fucker and he does pack that theater three times a year.

Vanity, Robin believed, was a sign of good health, in itself anyway not a bad sign at all. His own hair had turned gray prematurely. At Robin's fortieth birthday lunch, at the Co-op Diner, he had welcomed a guest with the safe remark, "I guess this is the big one."

"Now which big one is it?" returned the guest with sincerity. He thought fifty was a possibility.

That reminded Robin. "Hey," he said to Eliza. "I fooled the Guesser at the fair."

Eliza turned to him slowly, with heavy-lidded brown eyes, flecked with gold. Those broad, pale cheekbones you wanted to caress, you wanted under you. A silence fell around them. Everyone heard him.

"Hey, the Guesser," said Eliza's husband.

The Guesser was a man who could have been one of Robin's clients. He was a great, wasted hulk in his sixties or seventies, slouching on a stool in front of a plywood booth at the state fair. He was built like a collapsing crane—not a bird, but a well-digging crane, a building crane, folding into itself out of sheer misuse. He called out in a voice that was long and hollow like a rubber hose, "Guess your age within two years. Guess your birth month. Guess your weight within ten pounds or your money back." If he was wrong, you got your money back; in other words, the guess was free, if he was wrong. This draw was almost irresistible, somehow. As if you might be able to fool this Guesser or the next one right up until your dying day—maybe even then.

"Yeah," said Robin. "I got my kid to call me Grampa as we went by. Of course he overdid it a little. Grampa, grampa, grampa. But it worked just the same. Forty-eight, he guessed." Robin paused. No response. Surely everyone here knew his real age? "Four years too many," he added. "Point is, I fooled the guy."

"I have a Guesser story to beat that," said Eliza.

She leaned toward Robin and a certain perpetual sleepiness, some kind of reaction to years of turmoil, vanished from her face. Her skin glowed over her cheekbones. She looked directly at Robin, targeted him.

"Twenty-seven," she said.

They all stared.

"Yes," she said. "I pulled my hair back, and I had my son with me—and still. Twenty-seven."

She smiled at Robin. To have provided her with an opportunity to tell this story thrilled Robin; his heart hung out in space for a moment. She needed him, of all people, to know that life had not yet defeated her, that her face, sculpted by God on one of his good days, supported all the decisions she had made. The darkness under her eyes was just a touch. Her extra pounds, here and there—just a touch. Eliza's face came to life as she talked, then relaxed again, into that sleepiness.

But, thought Deena, observing the exchange from across the room. Suppose the Guesser was not completely craven. Suppose he rewarded himself, stuck up there on his stool, by making pretty women smile, or any woman he wanted to? Suppose when Eliza walked by the Guesser recognized her as a lady with some burdens that he could lift, and underguessed? Well of course that must have happened. How else could he say, to hell with this gig?

The Guesser reminded her of Yeats's long-legged bird. Symbol of longevity, brooding over the strange landscape of the fair. Passing out favors. How many women walked away feeling good and thinking, maybe I'll have another ear of corn after all! Plus I get my two dollars back!

She picked at the idea.

"Let's go see that moon of Anton's," said the woman next to her, the new professor, Molly, in a low, shy voice. This talk of the Guesser made Molly want to make a sharp remark, or escape the room. Either one.

"Let's," said Deena, rising from her lotus position.

Molly was pleasantly surprised at the effect of her words. There was a brief sorting out of groups: those involved in conversations seizing this chance to end one and begin another, those supine and lazy with food choosing to uncurl and get some fresh air. Everyone remembered babysitters, cars that might need to be started. Clothing had to be located. In heavy unlaced Sorel boots, in puffy synthetic moon boots, in felt Lobens with upcurled toes, people shuffled toward the door like preschoolers lining up for the next activity.

Then they were released into the night, where they found room, so much room. They crossed striations in the snow from the shadows cast by the spruce trees in the astonishing light of a full moon. They breathed deep and separated further, from groups into individuals. Perhaps this was why they lived in Alaska, winter nights like this one. Above them hung a jeweler's window. Anton howled softly like a faraway wolf.

At thirty-two Molly knew that she was probably the youngest person here—except for the children—and she was relieved to have talked about something as banal as the movies. Molly was still nervous, about this place and these well-established people who knew what they were doing. She'd have to get some solid work done for the tenure committee. She'd have to finish that damn treatise on Willa Cather. She knew that everyone assumed she was doing some kind of feminist evaluation.

Something about lesbianism maybe. That wasn't it at all. She thought that Cather was speaking for God in her books—she stood so far from her own characters, and she never played favorites. All of her characters were doomed, yes, heading for the finish. Annie Proulx, maybe, that's a modern writer who's like Cather. Annie Proulx, and maybe also Marilynne Robinson, but why? What was the similarity?

Anton howled again.

Molly wondered if there were wolves around here, if she would ever see one. Suddenly she felt the presence of things she had never seen. She was overwhelmed with a sudden vision of this dry snow-filled forest, bigger than anything she had ever imagined, extending around the entire globe, all through Canada and Russia. It was a great, strange landscape filled with languages, words, stories she'd never heard. And it was all cold and dry right now, the cold sucking the water right out of the air and the snow.

"Look," said Kate to the crowd as a whole. To the left a green glow began to separate itself into streamers of aurora borealis. One streamer then another unfolded to show pink on the underside, then more pink and purple, then a great bulge of pink and purple roared silently down a green ribbon like an egg swallowed by a snake. Molly wanted to shout. Her mouth dropped open.

Deena, to whom the aurora was as familiar and pleasant as a cup of tea, leaned back into Paul. He folded his arms gently over her chest and rested his cheek on the top of her head. Despite layers of clothing, he was suddenly intensely aware of her. He looked at the aurora but in his mind's eye suddenly he beheld his naked wife.

In her forties, Deena's insect-thin body had acquired an extra padding of muscle and fat—all over, not in one place; so her arms were shapely these days, her backbone lay between uplands of warm, toned flesh, and her bottom, which now pressed against his groin was rounder, bewilderingly attractive. Warmth grew on his skin. He thought that maybe, when the guests all went home, when Robert was snuffling open-mouthed in the next room, when Anna was curled on her bed amassing length and beauty even in her sleep, he would stop Deena from putting on her nightgown. He would lift it out of her hands and set it aside. When they were in bed, she would climb onto him, a white knee on either side. She would kneel over him and then...she would turn around and face away. She would put him inside her, she would lean forward. For a second Paul forgot himself. With the heat and movement inside his body a decade dropped away.

Twenty years married and he wanted this woman so much there wasn't room in his head for another; he wanted her tonight. Who's fooling the Guesser now, he thought. His hands tightened around her. She put her hand companionably over his.

Molly thought that sometime she would like to spend the night outside. There was something so tempting about the night, the moonlight, the trees. It's so cold and still and fresh, yes, or is it the silence? If I could only know this country. She had not expected to find in Alaska something so tempting to the lonely heart. Something in this empty wilderness that would go to work on her like a lover, would soften her guard, her own refusal to take part in the life around her.

With This Body

Penny Lampson drove from Fairbanks to Delta Junction three times a year to pick up goat milk yogurt for her skin cream business. She took along her son, Kelly, so he could enjoy the goats. The long drive, an hour and a half, was a little boring for him, but in the past year of troubles, Penny's wandering-through-the-desert year she called it, the round-trip was a bit of an oasis. Kelly was good at daydreaming; he could make the time pass. Just north of Delta they'd bounce two miles over a rough road to the Old Believers' goat farm, and he'd get to feed peanuts and grass to the goats while Mom loaded the gallon tubs of yogurt into her coolers and paid the Russian woman. The little Alpine goats were like dogs—mild and friendly, they liked people. Loved a scratch down the stiff fur of their handsome noses. They followed Kelly with his handful of peanuts all along the fence.

The Russian woman was younger than Penny. She wore a scarf around her yellow hair, a dress to the middle of her calves, and short rubber boots. She didn't meet Penny's eyes or make small talk.

This sunny October afternoon, the temperature climbed to forty degrees after an overnight cold snap. The birch and aspen trees around the corral were bare now, and the ruts of the muddy lane were crisp. It is so peaceful out here, Penny thought. Would I be happy living this way? The Russian girl didn't seem happy, until they finished loading the yogurt and walked slowly over to the corral to admire the animals and fetch Kelly.

The Russian girl held the belled goat by its collar and scratched the white forehead and smoothed back the brown-and-white ears. The goat and the woman looked at each other, and her expression, formerly flat and without affect, suddenly changed. Her face softened and her eyes focused tenderly, and she seemed to really be looking at her goat, in a way she didn't look at Kelly or Penny. Her wrists were bony and suntanned, her hands surprisingly wide and strong, her nails dirty.

She and Penny always said the same thing to each other. Penny would exclaim over what friendly, sweet animals they were.

The young woman added, "Yes. And good milkers."

"They do okay in the cold weather?"

"They keep warm together. We only have to keep them out of the wind."

Then Penny and Kelly would leave, to make a quick stop at the grocery store in Delta for an ice cream bar before the drive home.

This afternoon, when they studied the selection of ice cream bars, Penny's stomach suddenly turned over. She had to turn aside while Kelly searched for one. Her stomach rebelled at the sight of them in the dairy case—all those additives, chocolate sheathing and chopped nuts like angry studs, and swirls of artificial flavors like poison. She used to like stuff like that.

Something's wrong, she thought.

Halfway back to Fairbanks, the music on the car radio disappointed her. She switched it off. They drove in silence for a few minutes, and then Kelly spoke from the passenger seat. "Mom," he said, "why don't you smile anymore?" He was scared.

Her eyes filled with tears. Seven years old.

"Oh honey," she said.

When cigarettes and screwdrivers stopped helping, when they didn't anesthetize her one bit, Penny wondered if she might be pregnant. She remembered from eight years ago how the first indicator was a subtle but undeniable fickleness toward substances you were willing to take into your mouth. Jesus H. Christ, she couldn't bear it if she were pregnant. The divorce was only a matter of time, only waiting until she got her nerve up to insist on it, to say: Orrie, I mean it, we need to part, to be away from each other, and would you please agree with me 'cause I haven't the courage to do this alone!

After two weeks of trying to carry on as usual, she bought a pregnancy kit.

Thirty-eight years old, mother, wife, owner of her own business (Polished Shell Skin Products: homemade creams, footbaths, masks, and massage oils sold at farmers' markets and bazaars), and a member of the Fairbanks Chamber of Commerce for God's sake, here she was staring at a pregnancy kit like a high school girl. At the positive result she went blank. Utterly blank. Later on that night, she wept with horror.

The first time, too, eight years ago when she was pregnant with Kelly—she wept then, too. It was like her gut knew even then, there is something wrong with this direction you're going in. This whole life you have embarked on. This marriage! Why do you rebel, constantly, daily, why does every part of your body rebel every chance it gets? What is wrong with this life you've chosen for yourself except that you seem not to want it?

How could you not want this life?

It's this life or no life, for Pete's sake! *This is life!*

I love Orrie. I love everything about him, except for, oh God, so many things about him. It's not him, either, it's what he demands of me. What life demands of us. I don't know what it is! But I can't get back to the way it used to be, and nothing helps, nothing ever helps.

When, two years ago, she slept with another man, she thought that would be enough. A lover on the side. That kind of thing. Secrets and mystery and pleasure, off in the corner of her life. Over there, in a separate and private place where it wouldn't hurt anybody else. She didn't call it cheating. It was more like a pressure valve, a safety valve, a private life. She didn't know what to call it.

To feel lust down below, after years of mechanical routines with Orrie, well it felt like the Pentecost. A fire that woke her up. She thought, how could I say no, down boy, douse that flame of life, when I felt alive again, responded to sights and smells around me like a body should?

Why couldn't I feel this way with Orrie? But I couldn't. To want the touch of someone else who wanted me just as much—it was right and good and terribly secret and sinful and common. And turned me into trash.

And when Orrie found out, the guilt was so terrible that whenever he rolled into me at night, when he at least wanted comfort, I could give him that. I held him tight, I let him inside, and there was that time five weeks ago that we were back to front like spoons and we just lay there, with no protection, me holding him inside, and I don't remember him coming or anything. I should think I'd have known if he came. We just lay there. But that had to have been it. That's when it happened. Can guys just leak? Could Orrie have done it absolutely soundlessly and without motion? We huddled like two miserable lonely children who haven't a clue. I had no idea he was coming inside me!

But that had to be it because all other times we are meticulous. We're not ready for another kid.

Orland Lampson always kept the radio on to the country station. In the midst of his own misery, it would make him grin, to hear some country star's description of a bad day.

Big advantage to his days at the saw blade shop. In his previous job at the brokerage there was no country music allowed. A little talk radio, sometimes, down low. The pinstripe suits had to strike a tone and show urbanity, even in Fairbanks, Alaska. The patina of control had to be buffed.

Orrie's boss at the brokerage office arrived every morning with a twenty-four-ounce cup of black coffee, hung up his jacket, rolled up his sleeves, and lit a cigarette. Midmorning, midafternoon, he'd unwrap a Hershey bar. He sometimes rested the naked bar of chocolate on his function keys, he didn't care. He ate chocolate and smoked and kept the black stuff handy all day long. Sometimes he'd be consuming all three at once, even with a customer.

"Your fund includes Exxon," he muttered thoughtfully to one woman as he set up her new account. Anyone could tell from her Loben felt boots and her Patagonia clothes that she was greenish in her sympathies. At the mention of Exxon, she went, "Ohh—hmm!" and her hand came up to her mouth. Orrie's boss said, "Don't worry, their stock kept on climbing after the spill. They're doing really well." He had to set down a cigarette to enter data, and there was the Hershey bar, right on his filthy keypad, and the Styrofoam cup with that room temperature coffee in it bitter as solvent.

After Penny's investment ideas took some of the pressure off, Orrie got the hell out of that white-collar world. Penny's big idea, ten years ago, was to invest in beauty products. Her grandmother used to make them at home during the Great Depression. Penny said, "No matter how broke and confused people get, no matter what happens to the economy, rich and poor alike will always want a pretty little jar of ointment to put on their skin. It's a comfort that won't break you. The harder and more confusing life gets for people, the more they'll want it. 'Cause life is hard, and it's really hard on your skin."

They went through the ladies' magazines, *Vegetarian Times, Herbal Companion, Alternative Health,* and made a list. They studied up at the public library and then bought a few shares of natural cosmetic stocks: *Go Natural, Georgia Clay Beauty, Natural Therapy, Lavar,* and *Honeybee Skin Care.* And then Penny—all fired up—went into the business herself, at home. First she made soap with olive oil, hand cream with yogurt and wild rose petals, and a foot soak with juniper berries in it—a natural antiseptic, she discovered—and everything did pretty well. Now she had a dozen products. She made mouthwash for a while, but her recipe called for vodka, and the two of them kept drinking that up. Penny, mostly. She drank screwdrivers like water sometimes.

Polished Shell products were all for sale out front of the saw blade shop. In the front room, customers dropping off blades to be sharpened could study a selection of skin cream in jars, including a tough, no-nonsense hand cream for Alaska working men. Polished Shell did all right. It's partly in the packaging and labeling, Penny said, modestly. It's that momentary pleasure of opening a new jar and realizing, I am worth pampering. And for men, an extra little thought: my hands are softer *for her*.

Everyone needs a little softness, she said.

It's not like they were going to get rich. But they had started talking about building a vacation cabin up in the mountains, back when they daydreamed about a future together. Orrie got to leave that brokerage firm and go full time for the gig he really liked, which was sharpening blades. With the radio going, in the big, cool room behind the saw blade showroom. His partner, Jim, did welding repairs and made trailers for people to haul their snowmobiles and their ORVs when they went hunting. When he wasn't helping a customer choose a new Sawzall or chain saw, Orrie sharpened blades, any and all. Table saws, machetes, even garden shears.

He liked it that everybody, rich and poor alike, brought in their blades. The tree-huggers and the rape-ruin-and-run boys, all of them. Skinflints, trash-pickers, and guys with money to burn—if they had any sense at all they valued good edges. One thing about his customers: they had a conservative streak, intrinsic to their own personalities. A streak of obstinacy, that's what cheapskates have going for them. Some of Orrie's customers tended to remember the Great Depression—not personally, but they'd heard of it. They had a touch of nostalgia for a time when quality mattered in America and you never threw anything out. Guys even brought in blades they'd found in dumpsters.

His uncle back in Minnesota taught him the value of a good edge. His favorite uncle, Lute. Penny never met him. Orrie had suggested that name for Kelly, years ago, Lute Lampson, but Penny, who used to think of herself as Catholic, said you can't name a Catholic kid Luther. Orrie had never thought of that. Did it really matter? Geez, I suppose it would.

Only one time he felt uncomfortable at this job. A guy wanted him to sharpen an antique Samurai sword. Orrie didn't get it. What do you do with this, he asked, uncharacteristically. None of his business, really.

The customer was a small, tidy man, a pressed collar showing underneath his wool coat. Maybe in his twenties. A kid with a neatness fetish. Obsessive-compulsive, maybe. Dangerous. He cleared his throat and said, "I'm living up on the summit and there's been a bear hanging around. Frankly I plan to carry it with me when I use the outhouse."

"Why don't you carry a gun?"

"That seems a little unnecessary. I don't want to invite an encounter. I might be tempted to use a gun when I don't have to."

Sounded to Orrie like the kid really wanted to use this sword. Was looking for a chance. But he went ahead and sharpened the thing and then tried it out on his workbench. He looked around and saw his cheese and turkey hoagie, unwrapped, waiting for lunchtime. He couldn't resist. Raised the blade, brought it down. Exquisite! Again and again, he sliced until the sandwich Penny made that morning had turned into ribbons, crumpled shoelaces of turkey, cheese, and white bread.

There was something beautiful about a blade working so well. He and Penny had discovered the work of their hands, at last; she stirred skin creams, he sharpened blades. You'd think they'd be happier. You'd think. She didn't seem to mind sex; even if they were curled up to sleep, she wriggled and moved her bottom against him when his penis nudged the beautiful warm slope of her hip. Though after sex, there was no change. The sadness, the loneliness continued.

He thought of touching the tip of the blade to Penny's skin. To see it against her skin for a minute. He thought of how she'd listen to him then all right. She'd come alert. What a thought. He would never want to hurt her; he wanted to feel, once again, her respect for him. She let his penis inside her like she'd let in a little homeless wanderer looking for a home. That's not what he wanted, when he thought about it.

'Course when the homeless wanderer knocked at her door, he usually wasn't thinking too much. Glad enough to get inside. Any pretext at all. Maybe if she could see him touch this sword to something, raise it gently even over something of great value...even her white skin...he'd see the barbed wire of her animosity, that porcupine tail she was always flashing, go away.

As if he didn't have the right to be angry after what she did.

Let's not think about that anymore. Don't go back there.

Not submissive to him but tolerant of him. Couldn't she do that much. Just tolerate him. Let him vent around the house once in a while. Years ago he used to tell himself she sparked because she was a redhead. But sometimes, now, it was all sheer blackness, winter when it should be spring, her confusion and grief crowding him out of his own house.

He wanted to touch her skin with this newly sharpened edge because he loved her, and he thought about her first, in everything new. With this blade, Penny, I thee worship. I touch your skin, I pull away. I pull all the sharp edges away. I will always do all I can to pull all sharp edges away from you.

I do not hurt you.

With my body I thee worship, but is that what you want?

—

135

Penny had not been to a doctor in years, and her previous one had retired. She picked a good-looking lady doctor from the photographs hanging in the clinic lobby. But when the doctor walked into the examining room, smiled, sat down on the stool, Penny had to fall back and regroup. This woman wasn't even thirty yet! How can you deal with all these complications when you're not even thirty!

The doctor had black braids to her waist, shining brown eyes, a confident smile that went away when it was not returned, long, handsome, golden brown hands. She was a modern woman. She had it together.

This doctor, Penny thought, doesn't know her new patient is a wreck—a boozer, accidentally pregnant, shackled to the wrong man, makes a living buying goat's milk yogurt from a dairy in Delta Junction then selling it back to people with aloe and lavender and urea and propylene glycol stirred in, with a bunch of promises printed on the label. She believed some of those promises herself. But not all. Like with Kelly. She made promises to Kelly she couldn't keep.

"Why don't you smile anymore, Mom?"

At the doctor's confirmation of her pregnancy, the tears gushed instantly. Penny gasped in disbelief, again, in shock again. Tears just poured out. Not again. She looked down and shook her head over and over, no way to hide it. The young doctor didn't look chagrined. She looked serious and kind, and just waited.

"This is not supposed to be happening," Penny stuttered between gulps of air. "I can't have another baby. We're getting divorced. Past month I've been drinking. A lot. I'm not well. I can't have a baby."

There was silence.

"I can't deal with a—I don't want to be a single mother."

"Well, you're about six weeks. So you have the time to make a decision."

Penny stared.

"If you want me to help you, I will. I'd have to refer you, if you decide not to keep the baby. But I'll do that. Or, if you decide to keep it, I'll help you."

"How can you help me?"

"You're at the very beginning."

"My body's not ready for this at all. My life, my family's not ready."

"How many times have you drunk this month?"

"Uh. Four. Four times. Drank myself to sleep."

"As far as your physical condition," said the doctor, "your blood pressure is elevated, but I promise you, if you stop drinking and smoking, everything will be all right."

You can't promise me that, Penny thought. I could have a damaged child and sue the pants off of you. Wait till I tell Orrie what you said.

"I don't know what to do."

"You will know. Maybe you just have to find out what your decision is—it'll be there, inside you."

"Are you married?"

"No," said the doctor.

Of course not, Penny thought. A together person like you wouldn't make that huge mistake out of sheer loneliness, like I did. If that's what I did. I don't know what I did or where it went all wrong.

When she told Orrie she was pregnant, they just stared at each other. What followed was the strangest three days in the recent years of their marriage; they didn't speak to each other, not because of anger, but because there was nothing to say. For three days she went through her work routine, played checkers and Parcheesi with Kelly, made muffins with jelly centers for his second grade class. She stared at herself in the mirror. You? She thought. You're going to make a decision of this size and importance? Don't make me laugh!

She looked in the mirror at the woman who needed to make a decision and saw a ghost. Her cheeks were long and hollow now, lines etched on either side of her mouth. Kelly said it best. *Mom, why don't you smile anymore?* Her reddish blonde hair flew out at the ends like straws in a worn-out broom.

She could be pretty again if she put some real hard work into it. She could be a woman on fire, she could send out sparks. But God it was so much work. And what for, who wanted it, what being pretty led to—men coming after you with their loneliness and their demands.

Better put on a scarf and an ugly dress like the Russian woman at the goat farm. At that thought, despite herself, Penny almost smiled. That wouldn't last long. That would be one place Penny Lampson wouldn't last a week.

She waited for Orrie's input. Orrie's thoughts on the pregnancy. They weren't forthcoming. He said nothing. He walked around the house looking sad and serious. He did the dishes and with the first dusting of snow, took Kelly over to the sledding hill.

It was like something had landed on them. A meteor. Something out of the future. Something from outside their battling. Landed right on top and squashed all the puffery and vanity right out of them.

But every time she thought of what it really meant—a baby and little boy with a single mother, a baby never even to know a family life with two parents, born into separation and loneliness and withdrawal and, yes, poverty, because there's no way she could comfortably raise children on what Polished Shell brought in. The Lampsons did all right but only by combining incomes. They both had to work and now she'd have to work her ass off, she'd have to get a paper route or something else. Substitute teach.

Jesus the world wasn't fair, this baby never to know the hearty welcome of a happy family.

Why doesn't Orrie say something?

What does he want? I can use his opinion to steer by. Either for or against, I can use his opinion. But he's not saying anything. He can't. He doesn't know what to do. He's deferring to me.

She sat bolt upright, certain of it.

"Orrie." She shook him. "Orrie!"

Six in the morning. She must have dreamt the answer. Who knows. There was the decision, unwrapped, undeniable, as clear and solid as a pearl in the palm of her hand. As big and vivid as a dinner-plate dahlia.

"Hnnnh, what, what? Penny what?" Startled and wild-eyed, ready to take on a midnight prowler, he flailed and came upright. His limbs were still soft and hot. She liked it when he was soft and pliable early in the morning.

"Hey, I'm having the baby. So. The decision's made. We'll take it from there. We're having this baby. Whatever comes. See?"

"Yeah?" He stared at her.

His black hair was all spiked up and she saw the gray underneath. Gray just this past year.

"Yup. That's it." She smiled.

"Oh," he said. "Penny, that's great." He didn't say anything more. He didn't say *I thought you would*, or *that's the best idea*. He really had not known what to do.

She remembered, when Kelly was born, how awestruck Orrie was, filled with wonder, and something else—admiration.

She lay back down.

"Go back to sleep, now," she said, and pulled the blankets up to her chin, staring at the ceiling with new eyes. Where is it written what happens next?

"Oh, it's wonderful. I'm happy," he said, and his arm—heavy, pliable, limp—fell across her. "I'm happy."

Well, he didn't know the half of it. My having the baby doesn't mean anything but that. This doesn't mean we don't get divorced. Just because we're not going to fight for nine months doesn't mean we are going to stay together. We have one more thing to do before we part, that's what it means. We have one more thing to do. Or I do, anyway.

Orrie, don't get the wrong idea, she thought.

"We'll schedule an amniocentesis, because of your age," the doctor said, cheerfully, as if she thought it was something Penny would like.

"Why?"

"At thirty-eight, at your age...amnios are often routine. But no, there's no particular cause for alarm right now, none at all. Everything's normal."

"Then we won't do it. No amnio." After grim results from an amniocentesis, it would be decision time again. I'm done with that. I didn't make a decision just to be sent right back to make it again. No, no, give me a break. I just won't think about it.

The doctor looked startled.

Aha, Penny thought, I got through her façade! She's got it together but she wasn't expecting that! *I promise you, if you stop drinking and smoking, everything will be all right....Look, did you mean it or not?*

"Well, all right. I do think an ultrasound..." the doctor said.

"Let's do that, that's fine. That's great."

Orrie wanted to see the ultrasound, so he said he'd bring Kelly and come on over to the clinic from the saw shop at four o'clock, meet her there, but of course he didn't show. He didn't ever leave work undone. He could never say to himself, I better not start something new because I'm supposed to meet Penny in half an hour. Jesus. He wouldn't imagine doing such a thing.

And he could never resist showing off for Kelly around all the cool, dangerous stuff in Daddy's shop. So of course he was late, if he was coming at all, and for once the technicians at the clinic weren't late, and what was Penny supposed to do, hold them off?

Didn't matter, didn't matter. This was something she had to go through with. It was between her body and her child's body, it wasn't a matter for anyone else to deal with, she didn't need anyone else, she certainly, as it turns out, did not need Orrie. For the first time in her life, Penny thought, she really wasn't looking back.

There was a song in a movie... *Tender Mercies*, the movie was called. Robert Duvall strummed this tune on his guitar at a kitchen table. "I've decided to leave here forever," he sang. "Let me know if you're coming along." Then he winked at his new wife and said, "Not really."

But me, that is exactly what I want—to leave the old way forever. I don't know exactly what I mean, but that's the only way to do it. Get up and go. You can come or not. Why didn't I ever think of this before?

"Mrs. Lampson?" the technician called out to the waiting room. She was a thin, dark-haired woman in a tight sweater and stirrup pants.

"Yes," Penny rose and dropped an old *Kiplinger's* back onto the coffee table. She began a nervous smile, but the technician's lips stayed horizontal and clamped together. Penny abandoned her own smile. The technician was really that, a technician. A connector of wires and squeezer-out of cold gel, a person focused on a screen.

On the table Penny stared at her own rounding, bare tummy with surprise. It was beginning to pooch up like a new volcano forming. She hadn't taken a good look. It was too puzzling, too embarrassing, at her age; it was something you hid for as long as possible, hoping that people weren't eyeballing your thick waist. We think we're on a self-willed trajectory of some kind, but we're human, just like our own parents. Oh, fuck! This is just crazy, pregnant at my age!

The technician was very young and stone-faced. Absolutely nononsense. Not here to make friends. What on earth was her problem?

No problem. Just business. It's just business.

They said nothing to each other. Every few seconds Penny looked at the technician's face, looking for some expression of shock or alarm, as she moved her sensor around the greased dome of her new client's pregnancy. Maybe this was a deliberate poker face, maybe they're taught at ultrasound school not to give anything away, so as not to raise false hopes or frighten people or anything. Maybe she didn't like her job. Maybe she was heartily sick of other people's need for reassurance all the time.

It was cold in here and very dim, so that the image would show better on the screen. Penny looked at the ceiling.

The technician said in a flat voice,

"Would you like to know the baby's sex?"

Quickly Penny considered. With Kelly, she hadn't known in advance. That was fun. But what the hell, why not do it different this time? This is the last time. Why not try it another way?

"Sure, why not, let's have it."

"It's a boy," said the technician.

A new planet entered Penny's world. A star arrived from light years away. Awestruck at the telescope, she was Galileo. She was Eve. She turned her head and stared at the other woman through tears, her mouth fallen open.

"Oh!" she said. "Oh, Oh! A boy!" Her heart poured out in pure amazement and gratitude, and tears came down like a creek in the mountains, like a song from a thousand secret harps.

The door swung open and Orrie and Kelly stumbled in. Some kind of loud, nervous apology from Orrie about being late.

"Orrie! Orrie! It's a boy, it's a boy, it's a boy!" Penny cried, her voice playing along with her sobs like it was meant to be, like Gershwin wrote it that way.

"It's a boy! Oh, that's wonderful, hear that, Kelly? and Penny, I have the perfect name! Lute Guthrie Lampson. Not Luther, just Lute. Leave it there. Do you like it?"

"Lute!" said Penny. "Oh, that's a beautiful name. It's perfect. It makes me think of mountain climbers!" Orrie and Kelly were next to her then, staring at the screen, and the technician was trying to show them the baby's parts. Lute's parts. Lute Guthrie Lampson. Penny didn't try to look at the image, she couldn't make sense of it anyway, black and white squirls just didn't sort themselves out for her. It was like the duck and the rabbit puzzle or the vase and the crone. She simply couldn't see what she was supposed to see, so she wouldn't try. Why get frustrated on this day of days.

But she did see the face of the young technician whose left hand still rested lightly on Penny's belly. She wore a grin as wide as a barn door. All unwilling at first, she had joined the party. She had gone from stoic to soft, just like that. Let herself be affected! She wore a name tag, a plastic rectangle pinned to her tight sweater: Brenda. Brenda was laughing, in spite of herself, as if she was present at an actual birth. Something inside her had been startled into compassion. Brenda had the right to think: I'm good at this! Look what I did! Made these three people so happy!

Penny's arm was around Kelly, and her hand squeezing Orrie's as he leaned over her to stare at the first pictures of Lute Lampson swimming toward his family.

Without thought of any future, she fell into the present moment and looked around with joy. There might not be a future for Penny and Orrie. But for now life was abundant. Agony in the past had dug out this space between them, into which satisfaction dropped, a perfect fit.

Why, this is the happiness you're supposed to have. This is the now before all the decisions to come, the divorce and all of it, this is the now, this is it.

Nothing detracted from that day, ever, not even the divorce four years later when Kelly was old enough to punish both parents with his anger, and when Lute's round face and huge blue eyes showed the bewilderment of the innocent. An earthquake rocked the living room one day, and Lute shouted, "Mom, what's happening?" with the very face he wore during the divorce. Later on, he associated his parents' distress with a gathering storm, and spent one year screaming whenever the wind picked up. "It's a tornado coming," he would moan, and it didn't help to assure him, "There are no tornadoes in Alaska. No tornadoes here." He knew better.

But one day, when Lute was five and Kelly twelve, when the sky was still and blue, Kelly took the training wheels off his old bicycle, set Lute on the bicycle seat, and spent four hours with him, until the little boy could freewheel down the rutted driveway. They both wore grins that day, and Kelly never once showed impatience. Watching from the deck of their little rented cabin, Penny thought, a rosette for each of you. A badge of honor. We're still here. The surprises keep coming.

The Same Salt

The same salt that flavors
The table sweetens the breath,
Causes the blood to rise, spoils
The pilaf and brightens the smile...
   —Diana Der Hovanessian, "Salt"

MICHAELA

The approach to Eagle Summit is completely without landmarks. Blowing snow and white skies over the treeless dome wipe out any sense of location. It's impossible to know if the road lies before you or if you're about to drive over the edge. A young man operating the snowplow for the Department of Transportation drove straight when the road curved and dove off the road into white twilight. Those mustard-yellow behemoths are supposed to bring safety to this white chaos. But he died in the crash of his plow. After that they put up a couple of lines of safety poles on the approach to the summits. During whiteout conditions, it's all a driver can do to go a few feet at a time, losing one marker before spotting the next.

A winter drive up to the hot springs includes two of these harrowing summits in 150 miles. The driver sits forward and tight and no one talks much—but at last, with good luck, the car is back on solid ground in the village of Central, Alaska. Then it's a right turn and eight miles to Arctic Circle Hot Springs, a naked sprint across the ice into the hot outdoor pool, and a leap into green water with its hint of floating algae.

The frozen soles of my feet burn. After a few minutes of ecstasy, the mind loosens. I savor the fact that the three-hour journey is complete: we're here. I put a hand on top of my head and feel my hair crisping up like potato chips as it starts to freeze. When I sink below the surface, my hair sizzles. Through gaps in the steam I can see Polaris and the big dipper and even, in the floodlights, a snow-covered hill rising above the fence around the pool.

And then, as always, I start to think. I swear, I start to think when I'm in the middle of sex even, I go over and go over the past. First I think about the drive then about the things I left unfinished in Fairbanks. Then I go all the way back. The hot water supports me tenderly in the blackness while I regret my own thoughts, the direction I'm taking even as I take it, here we go again. And oh, Christ, for what purpose? All these years, I think I've been barking up the wrong tree.

I brought my friend Robin with me this time. We have a spiritual partnership, and we're affectionate with each other. She's good company, but it would be nice to have a man with me right now, to feel another naked human body in this heat, in this subversive place where the order of the world is turned upside down and everybody has the same secret (everybody has a cold crown, like the top of an iceberg, but below that a hot, willing, floating body, arms moving like a dancer's, legs loose and open).

But this, all these many, many years of thinking about the right way and the wrong way to be with a man. What a waste.

The man himself isn't the problem and isn't the solution. The problem is misdirection. Praise of a man, worshipping a man, that's not the problem either. That's a great thing to do, like for an hour a day. That's what love is, to look adoringly up at the strength of a trunk, the magnificence, the grace, the otherness—oh, no, the tree itself is not the problem, nor is the need to admire this guy. It might be the best part of me, this desire to praise.

Clouds of steam come together and part again. All of us in the pool are bobbing in someone's hot, sweet (well, make that sulfurous) drink. We're being stirred and then we're being left alone. Boundaries aren't fixed. I consider, at an irrevocable remove, what happened to my marriage: I see the swirling currents for what they are, and I keep getting these clear snapshots of what they were hiding.

For ten years I was married to Thomas Bernard Stone. And for three years before our marriage, I lived with him. And for a year before that I dated no one but him. And for a year before that, I liked him, eyeballed him, all that. So you see, it should have been a safe bet. It all foundered of course, on his toxic relationship to his work and my toxic relationship to alcohol, but *what was it* that steered us onto those rocks in the first place?

Something saved me from the relationship, shot me out of it like a foreign particle that never belonged there to begin with.

And something keeps turning my head around, forcing me to look back. A goddamn logical problem that I have got to solve. I can't keep it in my mind *not* to think about him, Tom, the way he used to be before I knew him very well.

RUDY

This is my second winter tending bar at the hot springs. Between this job and the others, working here and at the hospital in Fairbanks, I see a lot of familiar faces, and I'm not always sure where I've seen someone before. But I remembered her, that woman with the dark hair and the deep, bruised eyes.

I wondered at first but when she came downstairs into the bar at the Hot Springs Hotel after her swim, I knew for sure. Her hair long and wet against her face, it was like the time she came to the ER in Fairbanks. Her husband brought her in about 6:00 AM. She had fallen down their stairs, drunk enough to be floppy so he couldn't find any broken bones, but he couldn't be sure. Then she couldn't stop the heaves and he was afraid she had alcohol poisoning. They admitted her for the day, to take X-rays and give her an IV.

She was a surgeon's wife so she got good treatment and fast. Makes a little difference. A drunk is a drunk, but a surgeon's wife is also the surgeon's wife. Call it professional courtesy. Sorry, but it happens. I spent a few minutes with her, in the hospital. She made a deep impression.

Tonight she came into the bar, string of wet hair against her face like seaweed, and I thought, would we scrape her up off the floor tonight? Pull her drowned body out of the pool in the morning?

Swimmers get very thirsty after soaking in that hot water. But she didn't order a drink. She ordered a Diet Coke and a glass of water. I filled a bowl with pretzel sticks and took it over. She said, "Ah. Thank you." The salt would make her even thirstier. But pretzels are good for you, I've heard. I mean they aren't going to hurt you.

She didn't remember me. You wouldn't. You wouldn't remember every stranger in blue coveralls who cleaned you up, drew blood, checked your IV on one of the least pleasant nights of your whole life. But I sat with her for a few minutes that next evening while she was eating her first meal in thirty-six hours, two poached eggs. Guess she didn't remember that, either. Doesn't matter. You wouldn't expect your CNA to moonlight as a bartender half the year. Well this job at the hot springs isn't really moonlighting. This is another in a whole string of pearls. Glenn Miller. Because I like it that way. I like the freedom to move around. To think *well kiss my ass good-bye* when a supervisor pisses me off.

When I came back on shift at the hospital that evening, she was still there, moved up to a nice room. I took her vital signs and the orderly brought in a tray. I cranked up her bed and she looked at the tray. Could her stomach handle a little food? She lifted the gray plastic dome over the plate and looked at the eggs on the white toast and bent her dark head over the food and sniffed. Then she looked up at me.

She had these very dark, ready eyes.

You know, there's a time in everyone's life when they're ready. When they're willing to learn a lesson. She seemed ready, so willing to learn something that she even knew the lesson could come from anyone, at any time, even from the nurse's assistant she didn't remember meeting the night before. Because she looked at me like that, I looked back at her. You can talk with patients or not, it's not always necessary. I looked back at her. She made an impression.

"It looks good," she finally said.

I was like a lot of nurses in that we tended to keep our smiling to a minimum around alcoholism patients. You don't know quite how much smiling to do. Alcoholism counselors, they smile plenty, they're always breaking out in gut laughs. They know their stuff. And they're on the good side, the living side not the dying side, of the disease. But we humble certified nursing assistants, we don't know quite how much grinning is called for. So I didn't smile at first.

I said, "You want to give it a try?"

She studied the plate again and touched the packets of salt, pepper, sugar.

"Look at this," she said. She put a finger in her mouth and wet it, then she put her fingertip down on the tiny packet of salt and raised it to me. The salt perched there like a mortarboard on the head of a graduate.

"Salt kills you," she said.

We both looked at the salt, and I didn't know where she was coming from or going to with that remark.

148

"There's salt in this," I said, raising my hand to the IV bag and the solution that may have saved her life, ended the spasms in her stomach that very morning.

"So what do you do?" she said.

It seemed like an alcoholic's question to me, the kind of wallowing in unsolvable conundrums that they do.

I didn't say anything.

She put the salt down, opened the pepper, speckled her eggs and took a bite. A sip of coffee. She opened the salt and sprinkled every grain onto her food. She took another bite.

"Yeah, this is awfully good," she said. She looked up at me. "This is very good. What have I done?"

"Well, you were drunk," I said. "It doesn't matter what you've done."

"How can you say that?"

"I take it back. It would matter, if you had done anything that had to be set right, but as I understand it, nothing like that happened. You got drunk, you hurt yourself, you came to the hospital."

"I've hurt my husband."

"Well, now. You got drunk. You hurt him by being sick. Your suffering is what hurts him. What's this about how salt kills you?"

"Salt, it's one of those things that can kill you. So why do they bring me salt on this tray when I've just stepped back from death's door?"

"Do you have high blood pressure or something?"

"You don't even know!"

"What don't I know?"

"Salt's bad. Inherently bad for our chemistry. You shouldn't even feel tempted by it. If you really feel tempted, you're probably bad, too."

"Well I don't, much."

"Come on."

"If salt is bad, like you say, does it make you good to stay away from it? I don't think so."

"No, no, no. You don't understand. What's your name?"

I touched my name tag. "I'm Rudy."

"I'm Michaela. Do you order margaritas with or without the salt?"

"I take them as they come, Michaela. How about you?"

"I prefer not to be asked. I want the salt but I feel bad asking for it. God, it's funny, I'd love a margarita right now. How can that be? My stomach nearly turned inside out a few hours ago and my tongue is craving a margarita. How can that be? How can I betray myself all the time like this?" Her eyes filled with tears, those deep-set dark eyes. I was so far out of my league that I'd probably have been fired if anyone walked in, I could say the wrong thing and drive this poor woman further into her madness, and yet, there I was, the guy on the spot. You do what you can when you're on the spot. She wanted a human connection, after all, not a professional service.

I know that much.

The hospital gown was loose, had slipped down from her collarbone, and strings of her hair, long and unwashed and sweaty, lay over her white bones like seaweed. The thing you don't know is, are they on their way toward death, these drunk patients, or just coming back from a close call? Stepping into the coffin or stepping out? But she was eating now with some relish, scarcely pausing between bites.

"So how do you feel about salt now?" I asked, seeing she'd done a pretty good job with the eggs.

"It feels kind of like life," she said. "Like goodness."

"Maybe you can handle it," I said. And then I may have smiled. I was thinking, maybe you can handle this poison, where other people can't, but you can't handle the alcohol and I hope you can learn the difference between things you can handle and things you can't—but I didn't say anything more. I don't have much to go on, myself.

I looked at her now, across the bar, sucking the pretzel sticks before she crunched them. I got busy with some other customers and when I looked at her again, another woman was sitting with her, and they were laughing like old friends. Funny, when I saw that, the feelings that went through me. Like some really great story was not about to unfold after all. She had not come up here alone. She was just having a weekend getaway from Fairbanks with a good friend. Christ, maybe with a lover? They didn't look that way but you never know.

Tom Stone

I like to shoot some baskets when I get home in the evening, if there's any daylight left. Out there on my court I don't miss Mickey or anybody else. It's always been one of my favorite times of day. She used to call me in for dinner after an hour or so. I liked that too, her calling me in.

Mickey and I could have had a real good life together. We had a shared history. She was the heavens to me, the constellations in their heaven, everything fixed and flowing along, she was that, to me.

Tonight I came inside when it got dark and looked at the clock: eleven already, and I hadn't eaten anything. I got a few pretzels from the barrel and looked around for something to fix. I like these giant pretzels from the discount warehouse because they have no fat. Mick hated that I try to have a healthy lifestyle. She resented it. But it's not hard to avoid fat or to knock some of the salt off your pretzels when you've looked at as many plugged-up arteries as I have. When you've cut through so much body fat as I have.

I made some pasta and watched the sunset. May in Fairbanks. I looked down on the lights coming on in the city from my house on the hill. The city was like a sparkling lake, giving back the sunset.

When I think about Mickey, it's like spurs turning in my chest. She has no idea how much it hurts. I know I shouldn't think about her. I'm turning into a pillar of salt. I keep going back to it. The whole business of regret is pure poison. How can she live with herself? It's like a windmill of pain in my chest. I'm having struggles with my short-term memory. I can't remember to forget her. We aren't together anymore.

My mom died of Parkinson's disease. Her last two years were so awful, death was a blessed answer to her trouble. But I can't remember that anymore at all. It's selfish of me, but I can't remember how death put an end to her pain and her wailing, how the only alternative to death was more suffering. I have a selfish memory, a fucking disobedient memory.

Still after two years, I'm doing better. Losing Mickey may have left me a better person. Slower to anger sometimes.

Just a couple of months ago, just this winter, I looked up from my desk on the third floor, and down in the hospital parking lot the ravens were gathering. Absolutely totally frozen white outside, that afternoon. The three or four ravens were like letters of the alphabet on a blank sheet of paper. They were so alive in their greed as they flew up to the rim of the garbage dumpster. They were waiting for more ravens. Like letters. Just a few ravens do not a party make. They eat in gangs. They need each other. So they waited for a crowd; pretty soon there were ten or twelve guys out there, ready to eat.

Mick and I used to go up to the roof of the hospital; I liked to look at the view with her. Now I don't go up there anymore, no reason to, she never comes by to drag me away from work, as she used to put it.

My skull fracture in ICU wasn't going to make it. A truckload of pipe fell on him at a building site. He was sixty-two years old. Retirement set for the coming September. How short and sweet the best of this life is. I sat there looking at the ravens, and suddenly, when I was so full of hopelessness and grief for this world and myself in it, I began to feel like I was levitating. My skin started to prickle.

I looked at the snow and the ravens and thought about Mr. Creven in ICU whose life was ending, and whose wife wanted him not to die. My skin started to feel so different—it felt porous and prickly and alive, like information was pouring in, insight I mean, moving in on me. My skin wasn't walling me off, it wasn't armor. I got scared, but it felt like a good scare, and I held the arms of my chair and followed every movement of those ravens. I'm not mystical about ravens, but they were, after all, the only live things to watch out there. And just then, as I was at the height of this weird vulnerability, this kind of awful, open-pored acceptance of the whole world, Mickey walked in.

I turned around in my chair kind of slow; I didn't have the energy to break the spell even for her. "Hi," I said.

She stared at me. It was like I was made of butter. I couldn't move. She came around the desk and bent over me and kissed my cheek. "Oh, Tom," she said. She put some papers on the desk and looked out the window, as if to find what I was studying out there. I didn't feel sad anymore, or only sad; I felt different, a complex of things. Chemically different. Soft. I couldn't raise an arm to take hold of her.

She kissed me, looked at me, and seemed to be holding some sentences in her mouth for a few minutes. And then she left.

After awhile I looked at the papers. They were health insurance claims. She was seeing a psychiatrist. Well, that's good. I hope she gets the help she needs.

MICHAELA

The bartender here at the Hot Springs Hotel looks familiar. I've met him before, in some significant context. Like I was with him when something important happened. He looks like Harvey Keitel. He looks intelligent as hell, but I guess I could be wrong.

His skin is pocked, his hair kind of long and wavy coming out from underneath a baseball cap, he's quiet. Quiet people are kind of intriguing, they give off the suggestion that they might be intelligent. The way he fills orders is graceful, he holds several orders in his head at once. I've read about this. You are looking into the future when you do that, not studying the drink you're making at this moment but already looking ahead while your fingers do the job at hand. The brain is pretty fabulous.

I used to come up here to the hot springs a few times a year with Tom. This was about as far away from the hospital as I could get him. I was afraid, when Robin and I decided to come up, that memories would flood me and ruin things, but it hasn't happened, the place is too weird for that. Robin is my sponsee from AA, my first effort with the twelfth step; but mainly, I hope, we're friends.

I was telling her about barking up the wrong tree, and she says, so is there a right tree?

And I guess there is. You might say, God. That's what I said, embarrassing myself slightly. It felt okay, though.

What does the rest of the world think?

"It's like one of my tires is a little low, Robin," I explain. "And I'm correcting like hell as I drive. If I don't correct, I veer to the side, and in my case, I keep veering toward the past. I got to keep correcting, to stay away from him. After two years I'm still correcting. I have to quit hoping."

I think about that time I walked in on him in his office at the hospital. He was so soft, so quiet, so vulnerable in his chair. You could tell the meaning of life was sitting in his lap. I'd never seen him so available. I almost said, "Tom, if you'd been like this more often, I never would have left you." What was he thinking? What if I had said that, what if I'd taken his hand. It would have sounded like an accusation, and he would have bristled right up, or shook his head in anger, and the moment, whatever it was, the moment would have been destroyed. Not just for me but for him.

Robin is drinking club soda. We're in the bar because there's nowhere else to sit and have a snack in this place, except in front of the TV upstairs in the lobby, and a bunch of kids up there are watching a really dreadful movie in which Arnold Schwarzenegger gets pregnant, I kid you not. Club soda is an interesting drink because they add sodium to it—why, do you suppose? When we emptied the bowl of pretzels she waved it at the bartender, feeding her thirst with more salt, and sure enough, in a few minutes, not offended at all, he brought over a full bowl. Robin knows the ropes in bars. I'm not one for bars. I always drank alone. Oblivion was my goal. Robin's a party girl, an extrovert. I feel very safe with her. She lets you know her mood, what she's thinking. She's inside out, very responsive, and I feel very safe with that.

"We need to put some air in that tire," she says. "What you're saying is, though, like, don't be shocked by the force of that impulse to veer off course. But try to get back on the road. What's that word, not arrogant, that other word we use?"

"Complacent. Don't get complacent, don't ever kid yourself. It's mighty hard for such as us, Robin, to walk away from something we don't understand, from a problem we haven't mastered."

We look at each other, sucking our pretzels, because I've just said the magic words. The words we understand. It's not something we're ever going to master. We've got to turn our attention away, leave a big problem unsolved.

I look toward the bar and he's watching me. I'm not sure I like that. It's a little sordid, to be stared at by the bartender here in this place that hasn't changed a bit in years. It's sordid. But it's part of life. I wonder about him and I want to look back, but often men who are good looking turn out to be kind of dumb, and in fact what would a live wire be doing tending bar up here, the end of the road, in the middle of winter? The people around here are set in their ways. Who is there to talk to? Maybe he doesn't want to talk, particularly. Maybe he's taking a break from something.

I've dated five or six guys since leaving Tom, and not one of them holds a candle to him. For interest and intensity. For what I'm looking for. Whatever. Correct, Micheala, correct: get back on the road.

Robin says, "Do you want another one?"

"I really don't."

"Me neither. Vamoose?"

"Let's."

At the door he's leaning against the bar, and he looks right at me then from just a couple of feet away. He's got a baseball cap on. I can't take my eyes from him, it's not his looks, it's visceral: he reminds me of something important. And there's goodness connected to it.

"How you doing?" he says. "You doing okay?"

"Mm."

He's almost blocking the door, and he realizes it, so he opens it for us. And he takes off his cap. He's going bald on top! He showed it to us, to me, he showed me his baldness! An encounter of just a few seconds, and he's using it for this—to not hide something. It's a pearl on a string. He puts his hand on my shoulder as if to help me through the door. Go on through. A courtly shove. His hand is a correction; I like it. Taking off the hat, as if to say, if we had more time together, I'd spend it *not* hiding from you. That's what he's saying. Not with words.

Well, I doubt I'll follow up on this, but it feels good.

You know when you're alive, don't you? That's the feeling. When body and soul aren't at odds.

I put a hand on Robin's back, to stop her from getting away from me. I'm just getting a glimpse of where I have seen him before. Wait, wait. At least he almost reminds me of someone. Oh, this is going to bug me for days. It has to do with saving my life. It has to do with that: saving my life.

But my life, like any drunk's, was saved not once but many times, by many guardian angels. And finally I pitched in, by making my offering, my little offering of absolutely nothing. My absolute zero: take this, because I give up. And then the rewards started to trickle in, starting with that first meal of poached eggs in the hospital, four, five years ago. And I don't believe this is a unique experience, not even unique to drunks.

I give up on the bartender. Just can't remember exactly. But I will.

"Okay, move on," I say to Robin. I've still got my hand on her back and she's heading upstairs, like I'm a blind person and her body's my guide dog. We're going to have some sandwiches and then get back in the pool, maybe go up to the top floor late tonight and play cards in the little nook they call a library that's full of Reader's Digest Condensed Books and old *Scientific American* special editions and yellow paper-backs and who knows what. God there's nothing to do around here. You just have to stop wanting to do anything. You've got to slow way down, and just live in the way time ticks by, slow yourself down with a lot of hot dips in the pool, just sit around. Used to be, Robin and I, we killed time. We murdered the best of ourselves, along with it. Now we've got our secret jokes, we slow down with the best of them. We take a look around. We howl at the stars, or could if we wanted to. Raise it up and cast it out. Aaarrrrooooooo.

"What's that?" she says.

I howl again. I'm not completely without a sense of fun, for Christ's sake. It helps, to have a sense of fun. It makes a ladder you can climb. Every rung goes higher, higher. Though with a Jacob's ladder you tumble down just as often, and maybe that's the wonderful part. More of it is coming at you. You've got another day. Not some day out there out of reach either—you've got this day, the one licking your face as you open your eyes. And if you can find a few people who understand and tell them, too, tell them about the pratfall, simply and with honesty, they'll laugh too. Brightens the day. Picks you up a bit. Baby you got salt on your face and your lips are shiny—what you been eating?

Grace

One night in September Grace Elvey drove up her road and found her driveway swarming with firefighters and her house in flames. She got out of the car and walked forward, disbelieving.

"Your house is totaled!" called out a teenage girl named Missy, who lived next door.

Missy's mother leaped at Grace and took her hand.

Flames burst out in patches on the house, dull explosions. It was a cold, damp night. *An odd night for a fire*, she thought. A strange, loud, continual noise, the hoses and something else, a crackle like the radio turned up too loud, filled the glowing bowl where her house used to be.

But her husband's shirts were inside that house. And his guitar, his wisdom teeth, his raven feather, oh his books. Two years since he died and there were things she had not touched in that time.

"Wait," she cried, and took a step forward.

Quick, make a list. The raven feather—there must be so many things like that—all but forgotten things she lifted out of the flow of years and set aside. And no list of them, no catalog. At the thought of so much vanishing in a night, she felt a sense of wonder. "God—" she started to say, surprising herself.

The firefighters moved around like hard-shelled bugs in their green coats. One end of the house had turned to velvet now. And leaned in on itself. You could see through the bedroom windows. You could imagine someone trapped inside, diving out. Grace stood with Missy's mother, gripping her hand, openmouthed.

She thought of the paint-by-numbers sets in the closet. A secret habit, something to pass the time. There were several shoved under the couch, too. Had she ever showed them to anyone? Oh God, she thought, I hope they burn up—how awful to have them dug out, saved, when other things, the couch itself and the living room and books and other things, are gone.

Was it the chimney? Something caught fire inside the chimney? Grace always had the chimney cleaned out, but not yet this year. She tried not to let things get away from her. She tried to be a careful woman, with no habit of leaving the stove burners on or the steam iron plugged in. She knew, standing there in the street, that she was without fault. This thing flared up because of life, because of chemistry, not because of any tragic flaw in her personality. Like when her husband died. He was in fine health, and then he was gone. What we think of as fine health held a strand called mortality. No fault in his diet. Not her fault. It was just out here—this complicated, deep current of life. We don't know what's in it. It's complicated, it's huge, life is. Takes people away. Takes a house. What did I do wrong? Oh God what did I do?

The cul de sac where the neighbors stood, watching the fire, was deep with sodden birch leaves. The neighbors were awed and gentle, except for Missy and a few others, on whom the fire worked like a stimulant. Missy couldn't help herself. Nonetheless, Grace wanted to slap her when Missy turned and said, "Wow."

—

Spices. One thing Grace couldn't bring herself to throw away was an outdated jar of coriander or oregano. She had boxes of allspice and cloves from the 1960s, and now that she thought about it, that was many years to have passed—a generation or two—time for a whole revolution, time for Columbus to have discovered spices in the first place, or whoever did. It was Marco Polo, maybe. Books. Look it up in a book. Black and crumbling, holding their shape like a timed joke. Books—touch them and they disintegrate.

The next day an insurance man gave her an inventory form. But why would I want to replace old spices and how could you ever replace a book collection, she thought.

It's not the things you can replace that matter. Everyone who knew Grace or read about the fire sent her something soft and warm to make up for a lifetime of possessions, to ease the ache. Instead of old spices and old love letters, old things from a not always sweet married life, she now could turn her attention to the boxes of afghans, sweaters, socks, and mufflers that inundated the neighbor's house where she was staying. A dozen pairs of army surplus green socks.

Grace sat down in front of the inventory form and a star of pain burst inside her as she began to read the list of household possessions line by line, room by room. There was a very small space for books. "Attach more sheets as needed," the insurance man said.

Furniture. Appliances. Paintings—surely she wasn't supposed to list her own. She folded the papers and ran the side of her hand down the fold, again and again, and pushed it away, across the desk, like a plate of fatty meat in the restaurant when you're suddenly full. She picked up a letter that had just arrived from her oldest son. He was coming to Fairbanks to see her, he promised. Words on a page—something to save, something to own. Once she lived a life as complicated and tracked up with things as anyone else's; now she was captain of four boxes of donated warm things and one letter. So!

She remembered the one velvet-lined drawer in her ancient jewelry case that held her husband's wisdom teeth, broken because the dentist had so much trouble digging them out, and Edward had been sick for three days afterward, dizzy from pain medication, and in that drawer were the children's baby molars, too—she just tossed them in, clean and pretty from soaking overnight in the jar of water next to a child's pillow, replaced by a dime or a quarter. She looked at the box of sweaters next to her, in the Goldens' underfurnished guest room, and thought: what I'd give to see something really strange. Like a handful of broken teeth in a velvet drawer.

Or a box of spices from 1962.

Or Edward's records, bootlegged Bob Dylan and scratchy, ancient recordings of Leadbelly, and the first Steppenwolf. And the silk robes he brought back from Vietnam. Heavy silk, falling over her legs like water. Edward opening the robe, or she letting it fall open, that time she sat back with her legs open and let him see her, really see her, let him look, that time. It all comes down to one memory at a time.

Her knees up and the lights on and the sky outside the bedroom window, and Edward's face—so kind, so willing, it was goodness.

What would the replacement cost be for three silk robes? Another war, a soldier prowling strange city alleys thinking of silk opening to show him white knees, white legs, dark hair, parted, yes, he parted the hair.

To look, to touch, to inventory.

She was staring across the room, living inside that moment again, but now she looked down at the desk, at Howard's letter, and she thought that she had no control at all over her thoughts anymore—this fire was turning out to be like Edward's death after all. She tried to take things in order. She had tried that—especially after Edward died—to cut every project in half or quarters or bits and do first one bit then the other. One little piece at a time.

But now she couldn't do anything. Just like when Edward died. She would start dreaming. And the dreams would lock her in place at the kitchen table, drenched in the smell and taste and weight of Edward and the depth of his voice, the hoarseness.

He was thin when he came back from Vietnam. No, not really thin, but just not the great stunning lout her loneliness had made of him. The skin on his shoulders, and where it sloped to his breast, was pale, mottled, tight. Almost transparent. He grew a beard. She put her mouth in the beard. Her mouth against his bearded face. Deep, like a jungle. She liked that, a mouth full of hair. Then his eyes lit up and he took her face in his hands and said, so close their lips were touching, and he smiling all the time, "Wife-to-be. My unwed wife."

She wanted to go on loving him. Watch him grow old, white in his hair and new expressions on his face. Maybe noticing her again. Looking across the room, marveling. But truly he had become a bit disappointed, bored with her. Hadn't he? Grace was so quiet and placid, so linear, he used to say. One step at a time. Don't leave anything out. You might regret it. You might get a B minus. He'd always smile and touch her shoulder gently when he teased her that way. She'd put her hand to his neck and tug at a spike of hair in return. Or they'd smack each other's bottom, when no one else was around. She was happy, didn't he see.

Edward's raven feather. He stopped going to Mass when he got back from Vietnam. They were teaching in Sitka and he prowled the beach, watching the gulls, eagles, and ravens. He read out loud to her from Native mythology. He decided that Raven was the creator. She thought it was touching, that he had simply made a substitute, like Equal for sugar, or something—one creator for another. Why a creator at all, she wondered. Why not just a sense, a flow, a will to live, a rhapsody of desire, why not just gravity, or wings? Why a master intelligence behind it all. Why not the wonder of molecules attracting each other to create, say, a doorknob?

The raven feather was many-textured, smooth as silk, then fractured and rough, black to blue from the quill outward. Edward said, once, looking at it in the cabinet in the living room, "I always want to have things like this around me." Just suddenly, out of the blue, a statement coming from a conversation he was having with himself.

She was the one who saved the boys' drawings and paintings and earliest scribblings. Howard and Carl. One a steady, quiet English professor, linear like his mom, wrote poems that way—scratch by scratch, word by word, every morning from seven to nine.

The other a mountain climber. Couldn't get far enough away from flat earth. Although Carl was the one who aborted his Himalayan climb when the Sherpa got sick. And sat with him in a tent on the glacier for two days until help arrived. If you had to depend on one person, it would be good if that person was Carl, who could turn all of his restlessness to stone when it was necessary. And hold your hand.

But, best not to depend on anyone. A nice enough moment, a moment of dependence could be; but best not to stay there. Stay independent by doing your job. And the job now is to take the inventory, fill out the form, and get your money. If your house burns down, you fill out the form. Just like anything else in life: if you get a job, you show up; if you have a child, you stop running around; if you fall in love, you take off your clothes. Like she did, when she was twenty, with Edward. In a converted school bus parked in a meadow, after they met at a funeral. Paisley curtains at the window. She and Edward, sneaking off. They laughed when they collided, their grins collided, the lies evaporated. There was only the truth between them. No more fancy stories. She was so scared, but something took over. She saw that moment. She took his hand.

Edward, what got into you to go and die?

Personal possessions: teeth, feathers, handprints in plaster, Carl's hand when he was three, even then it was a big hand, long fingers digging into the mixture of flour and salt and water so that it didn't come out right at all. She scolded him. Imagine that! Scolding a three-year-old for not cooperating, when it was she who mixed up that tempting goop, seized his hand and pressed it into the stuff, all excited and happy at the thought of the souvenir she was making. And his pleasure at the sensation and his curiosity took her by surprise, so she yelped at him. And scolded him. And saved the plaster cast with its extra deep fingertips as a reminder. Of what? Of whom she was, a mom wild with eagerness in her own right, making a plaster cast as if to prove to the world, I had a three-year-old once. Hold still, damn it, Carl!

Cost of replacement: no, thanks.

Why did I save all these things, when the memories hurt so much?

Howard arrived from Juneau. His smile, soft voice, wild black hair nearly broke her heart. He was lovelier every time she saw him.

Such a big, tender smile. At first he wouldn't let her carry anything, or drive the car, or open a door.

"Howard," she said. "I live alone in Fairbanks, Alaska. I can open a door."

But then she heard in the air, you *lived* alone. But look how you've screwed up. Your house burned down!

He brought his suitcase into the guest room to unload presents—oh no, a handknitted sweater, a Sony Walkman—how silly!—and something special, wrapped in paper. It was a red sweatshirt, with two birds—eagles—painted on it, in black and gold. It was beautiful.

"Why, thank you," she said, feeling awkward. The birds were on their way up. Soaring up. Two big birds covering the shirt. Howard was her cheerleader. You can do it, Mom, here you go! "Thank you," she said. He expected her to come back to Juneau with him. "Just for a bit," he said. "Or as long as you like."

They went to the remains of the house. It was her second visit. She thought she was used to it.

But with Howard there, it was different. While he walked delicately around the perimeter, she stepped across the black waffle that had once been walls, floor, and living room, and for just an instant she felt the great heat of the fire. That first cold night, when the firemen came, she felt no heat. But now—she felt it—that oxygen-eating wall of flame.

The killing smoke. And she knew that had she been at home, she would have died.

Grace started to shake. The walls of her house had returned to what they truly were, just wood, growing in a forest, dying, disintegrating. In one night, years of human pettiness were annihilated—never existed. Because of combustion. That's all it took. Against that fact of the universe, Grace was nothing at all.

She hugged herself and felt nothing but bones, ribs, a hollow rib cage. She had escaped with her life for now only because she wasn't home. Nothing here had escaped. The ground all around was blackened, crisp, stinking.

She looked at Howard, knowing that for all the horror he felt at this sight, he was also absorbing every detail. He would store it and write about it. Poets were worse than scientists that way, observing everything, setting aside their pity. Until later. They figure out how they feel about it all later on. I must have been in shock until now, she thought. I could have died. Nothing is left. There is nothing here. She backed away from the site. She sat down in the car with the door open, drinking in fresh air. I was in shock, she realized. I am not now. Take notice, Grace. A fire came through here.

"It's the money that really matters," she told Howard. "I'm having trouble with these forms. One simply loses things, that's life, but I can't go on without a settlement."

"Let's do it together," he said. "Line by line this afternoon. We'll go down to the bakery and do it there." The poet in him knew how to buckle down to work, how to fasten himself to a chair and hold the posture until a line or two was written. He could do it when he didn't care. That's what made him a poet. He could do it when he didn't care, because he had faith that it would make a difference.

Carl, on the other hand, called her from Colorado and couldn't think of anything to say. She knew that he was looking out a window as he held the telephone. She didn't know why he was like that, but she understood, for an instant, the impulse. Looking out the window, wandering off.

In the restaurant with Howard she couldn't get up and do something else, she couldn't say, "Let's stop for now." They faced each other
across coffee cups and pieces of cake, across the piles of insurance
forms, and they worked like two paid employees getting through to
five o'clock. Her furniture, her appliances, her dull and standard clothing. "But winter clothing," said Howard, "that's expensive, important.
That's premium, Mom. Antiques? China?"

"No."

"None?"

"There was that platter we served turkey on. And some old silk
robes from Vietnam, but really they weren't old. Just made for soldier
boys in 1965."

"Anything else?"

"Paints."

"Paints?"

"I took up painting a couple years ago."

"Gee Mom, I never knew that."

"It was a silly thing, I guess."

"Paints. Oil paints?"

"Well...as a matter of fact, yes. A very nice set. I guess I was a little
shy about it."

"That's terrific, Mom. Let's replace them right away. Did you have
an easel?"

"Yes." She put her palms around her coffee cup. "I'd even finished
a few. Still lifes, mostly. It was really quite pleasant."

"Did you take lessons?"

"No. I painted from the inside." She touched her chest.

"Did you ever show them to anyone?"

"Honey, I was a little bit embarrassed to do that. Put down—oh,
two hundred dollars, maybe."

"You sure? To replace all that? How about four hundred?"

"Okay. That's good. Four hundred."

She sat back in the booth and took a deep breath and looked out the window. There could be a point to this, after all.

They were on the beach at Sitka again—that is, she was there, and Edward was there, too, but they weren't together. She was walking on the surf-pounded stones, looking down for treasures like she always did. She looked up suddenly and he was coming toward her. Her heart stopped. He was advancing; they would touch; he was coming for her. But why was he dressed so funny, in an orange parka and a turquoise hat? He was coming toward her, though—at last!—but then, as he neared her, he smirked. And walked by. Without any hesitation in his gait. He looked at her, and smirked. He didn't even reach through the distance between them. He laughed in recognition, and walked by.

She woke up stunned.

She flew back to Juneau with Howard. For a while the warmth and glitter of the capital city would be an entertainment. The narrow streets winding up the mountain from the harbor were full of interesting shops, even a used bookstore.

Howard's wife, Leah, the subject of many of his poems, taught music in a downstairs studio. She was Hungarian. Their home was so cosmopolitan; Grace always liked to explore the bookshelves, the mantle, the dining room at her leisure whenever she visited. There would be something odd, something graceful, everywhere you looked—paintings, sculptures, pottery. Edward used to say that Leah was a hard nut to crack. Grace just reminded him that Leah came from another place. She was European—culture, to Leah, was a thousand years old, not a mere hundred.

What Grace noticed about Leah's house now was stuffiness. She herself wanted to be outside, on the move, walking up and down the mountain, prowling the beach. Bears were attacking garbage cans in the alleys. They warned her to be careful, not to wander off up the mountainside.

"I'm just going to pick out a few things to furnish my new house," she said. "Try to gather some ideas."

"Can I drive you somewhere?" asked Leah.

"Oh, my, no, what a luxury it is to walk in such a pretty place," Grace insisted. "You know, Leah, losing so many things..."

"Yes?" Leah held her head to the side, looked at Grace with tenderness. Grace thought, this girl's parents and their parents lost more than I can know, to world war, to revolution, and I'm going to lecture her?

"Well, it just makes you want to pause for a while, that's all."

What she had begun to say was, it makes you want to stop collecting things. Why gather up these objects and pretend they mean something? But here Leah was, the child of refugees, living out the true meaning of loss, the true and deep consequence of having nothing left. Me, Grace thought, I'm just an old hippie, that's what I've become. A straight, bereft hippie.

Walking down to the harbor, she didn't see any bears but she noticed the ravens. Flapping between buildings, perched on dumpsters and pickup beds. Big, bearded creatures. They'd flap and quork and go into a graceful soar that reminded her of a clown on ice skates. Somersaulting backward over a barrel to show you how clumsy he was, how artless: then suddenly flying on one foot in a graceful spiral across the rink. As if to say, the joke's on you now. And somehow, she thought, it is. The joke's on all these two-legged animals unable to get away from their own rubble. The ravens descend for lunch then they're off again. But we're here, all the time.

You could walk away from the boat harbor just a bit, along the beach road. Just enough for the wind to sting your face. The water, the mountains, the trees, the shrieking gulls assailed her. Here was a life she hadn't lived. A few years in Sitka, but they never owned a boat. She was busy with small children; Edward was making a living. It never occurred to her to cut loose and explore this strange, romantic country—all its quiet waters, all its coves, all the different sounds. God what they had missed. It was so rich here in Southeast, it made you cry.

And now she could start over. This was her chance to reinvent. To begin again. What shall I begin with? Oil paints. Real paints, and one of those painting knives you use to gouge out a lump of color and smear it onto the canvas. She knew how to frost a cake. She'd paint the same way.

When she began again, this life wouldn't be shared with Edward. Wouldn't be shared.

She closed her eyes and the wind washed her cheek, a gull screamed, and the city made its hum. I am alone, alone, she thought. I am finally alone. What shall I do with solitude? What shall I do in this emptiness? To work so hard to coax a smile from a man. And then in an instant he's in another world. He's not in this one anymore. And you just keep sticking your fingers in the hole where he used to be.

Heading back to Howard's house, she passed the used bookstore. Aha—if anyone ever had an excuse to buy books. She pushed open the door and went down a dark aisle. She came to a table piled high with remaindered art books. Nudes, flowers, seascapes. Here was a naturalist's life work—detailed flowers in pale watercolor, with no background, no context at all—just the flower hanging out there in space. Not for me, she thought.

She opened a museum catalog, from an exhibit somewhere of European ceramics. She turned the pages slowly, staring at collectibles that were centuries old. Suddenly she froze. A harlequin looked out at her from the book. Took direct aim at Grace Elvey. His face was white, his shirt made of triangles of orange and white, his pointed cap was turquoise. His knees were turned out, heels in, one leg raised as if about to stamp the ground. Or was he dancing? An ugly posture, an affront, a joke.

And he stared at her. Where had she seen him before? People bought this thing, paid money for it, craved it—why? Just to be accused, day after day, by this leer? Who is this creature?

She flattened the book out on the tower of remainders. She couldn't take her eyes off the harlequin's face. This, this creature was Edward in her dream. Yes, this was Edward. Stopping in his passage to eternity to look back at her, trapped in her loneliness, in her stupidity. But no, this wasn't her Edward—this was a fragment of clay. A dust catcher.

What is it? What do you want to tell me?

Her heart pressed against her breastbone. She was suddenly filled with pity for the poor fifty-three-year-old widow who had lost all her belongings in a house fire just a few weeks ago. Poor thing, she thought, poor thing, and suddenly, like frosting on a cake, like sunlight touching the beach, her eyes filled up with tears.

She walked outside and up the street, toward the mountain, toward her son's house. There's a joke being played on me, she thought. We don't know everything. This is a joke, and I can get it, if—if I can do what Edward is telling me to do. I can find the crack in the world and get out of this pitiful little box of treasures. Edward, are you out there?

She saw someone give her a strange look—an old lady with a wet face, talking to herself, belted into a borrowed man's coat. Feet flat against a street so steep the backs of her calves were stretched to their fullest. "There's where we have to go! Up there!" Edward used to call back to her when they went hiking—it was a joke. "Beyond that mountain! Back beyond the farthest ranges!" he'd holler, a terrycloth dishrag tucked under his baseball cap to keep the sun off his neck, so he looked like someone from *Beau Geste,* or *Kim.*

She would be too tired to laugh by then. She'd just stand there and feel good. What would he be looking at now? She raised her eyes to the buildings and the mountains. Look up, Grace, look where you're going, how lucky you are. To be seeing that. That mountain, that black bird looping about. She let her eyes follow a raven on a course between two state office buildings. It swooped below the tops of the buildings, into a long narrow gap, turned its head, and looked at her. Then, when only she could see, of all the people in Juneau, the raven did a midair rotation. Breast up to the sun, wings slicing at the earth.

She almost missed it. Look what I can do. Then he was up, over the top of the building, and gone.

"Edward," she said.

Her fingers curled around the handle of an imaginary painting knife. I understand, she thought. As the crow flies. Ha! We don't know how they fly when no one's looking. I bet they explore their element from top to bottom. They dip in and out.

She turned around in a slow circle, looking for more ravens. She walked backward up the hill, looking at the rooftops and the water beyond. They live in the whole sky, she thought. No reason not to. No reason not to inhabit the world. Nothing to do but live. From top to bottom of my life. They'll say, "Why are you doing this now, Mom?" and I'll say, "Because I haven't done it before." Why not? What else is there to say?

Ravens diving, ravens looking at you. Looking for a wife, a meal, a human being to tease. Yes! And she suddenly understood—who cares how late in life the understanding came—how many strange worlds touched her own, broke into her own, offered her a glimpse of things that would enrich her, no going back, if she would only look. Only look.

Psalm for Anabel

Anabel Hughes, age sixty-seven, one leg lost to cancer and four of her own twelve children underground, still wanted to dance when her cousin from Galena stepped up to the microphone and swung into "Jambalaya." *Good-bye Joe, me gotta go, me oh my oh.* Anabel's right foot rocked heel to toe, toe to heel, on the footrest of the wheelchair. *Me gotta go pole the pirogue down the bayou.* You could dance all night the way Hudson played Hank Williams, a little slow and offbeat. A crowd had turned out for the Athabascan Fiddlers. Long tables, pushed together in a big C around the stage, were nearly full of residents struggling to sit upright in their chairs. Over by the fish tank was a table set with shamrock cookies, green punch, green beer, and popcorn. It was Saint Patrick's Day at the Fairbanks Convalescent Center.

Lucerne, a nurse's aide in a brilliant lime green blouse, pushed in the gurney with a young man who had some kind of wasting disease since he was born. He was curled like a pretzel, and when she'd lean down to him, he'd open his mouth in a happy roar. His bare feet, one on top of the other, were soft and uncalloused as if he'd never walked on them. Lucerne began to rub the young man's arms and shoulders, once letting the back of her right hand touch his cheek. The fingers of her left hand tapped the bars of the gurney, and you could see her lime green fingernails. A gallon of black cornrows spilled from a barrette at the back of her head.

She wants to be dancing, thought Anabel.

When Anabel was seventeen, Saint Patrick's Day fifty years ago in Galena, Alaska, most of the young men had gone to work for wages in Fairbanks or Anchorage. The war meant wages for everyone. But soldiers came to the village, and they had such a dance with the fiddlers who were still at home, and there was a redheaded soldier who danced with Anabel. He had a crew cut the color of new copper wire and arms like she'd never imagined would hold her. Arms like peeled white spruce logs, arms like the river ice she stood chiseling for hours in January to open a hole for whitefish. Steel. He spun Anabel in his arms and her black hair—so black it was blue in those days, glossy and straight as a raven's wing, oh she was proud of her hair!—flew across her back like the wings of a plane. And he smiled to have the best chicken in his arms and proud of himself no doubt. Wherever he came from, they were used to dancing. Every time her skin felt those arms of his, felt his leg or chest against her, moving her around like he knew what he was doing, she wanted to laugh for joy and for pride too.

She was unthinking in those days, not a care for the future—young people today, they give themselves so many terrible worries, all the time fretting about their drinking and their Doyon stock and their dividends and their new snowmachines. One thing about a war, it kept you from thinking about the future. A war so far away it didn't seem real.

Oh but she was careless in those days.

The man across the table from Anabel, a tall man with nothing wrong with him that you could see, was struggling with a saucer of popcorn and a paper cup of beer. His fingers were long and slender, but he might as well have been wearing gloves, he had such a hard time getting hold of the popcorn. When he finally palmed one puff to his mouth, his lips went toward it in a way that made Anabel think of a moose going after aspen buds. The thought pleased her enormously, and she worked so hard to hold in a laugh she almost felt seventeen again. He didn't do much better with his cup of beer. It was a long trip from the table to his mouth.

It surprised her that they brought in beer even though it was Saint Patrick's Day. Alcohol had taken two of her own children, had wiped out so many. Her cousin, Hudson Carew, up there on the stage gave it up years ago, that's why he was still here. At one time when they were young, she thought she might marry him—and here he was fifty years later, sturdy and grinning and still playing his music. Alcohol cut down a lot of their family and their friends, cut them down like a machete. More of her own people lost to alcohol than in the world war or all the wars that followed.

But then, the beer reminded you that this convalescent center wasn't a mission, thank God, this center was a home. People lived here. A real home—for some the last home they'd ever have. Anabel would be going home to Galena next month. Missing leg and all, Anabel was better off than some here. She still had sensation in her toes. Between her legs. A decent bowel movement could still take her mind off any trouble. Not like the girl Vicky there by the door, in her electric wheelchair. Vicky lived next door to Anabel in the Birch Wing. She broke her neck sledding. Now she couldn't stand, or talk, or move her arms. The aides moved them for her, twice a day.

"Ready for some dancin', Vicky?" Lucerne would call. "All right girl, let's slide!"

Vicky could press her chin against a keypad to write letters and start and stop her VCR. She was only forty, and on her closet door was a full-length poster of someone named Fabio, who posed for the covers of novels. Fabio looked like the redheaded soldier except instead of a crew cut, he had long blond curls like a girl. The rest of him was the same.

A family came into the dayroom—a father, mother, two small children, and a teenage boy. The sad, shocked family visited Anabel's roommate nearly every day. They couldn't believe their grandmother could be taken by a stroke. They questioned the aides and the nurses like there was something somebody could do, if only the right questions were asked, like they were at a Doyon stockholders meeting. The father reminded Anabel of Mr. Rogers on television. Except he was grim. His face was pale and sharp, with a thin cleaver of a nose, and his hair was black and greasy.

The mother led the two smallest children to the table of food and punch, while the oldest son, the one the mother called her "spiritual son," sat down across from Anabel, his face turned away from the musicians, and opened a copy of *The Celestine Prophesy.* He looked like his father, except his hair was long, and his eyes were focused on something only he could see.

Anabel knew what the mother meant, calling her boy spiritual. Anabel had a spiritual son once, too. A quiet one who looked into things, deep into them. Paul.

Paul Hughes stayed thin no matter how much he ate. He thought about things. He lost himself in dreams. She came around the corner of the cabin one spring day when he was just thirteen, and surprised him. There he sat on a wooden box, surrounded by the ridged, filthy snow of late April, two rabbits on a tarp in front of him. His knife was raised to slit their bellies. He tested the knife on his glove and then touched it to one of them, pressed it into the fur and then, this just like Paul, he started to think. He looked up into the distance and waited, and when he heard her footsteps, turned and looked at her with eyes as deep and dark and faraway as holes in the river ice. What did he see? Looking at his mother, after a few seconds, his eyes returned to normal, he recognized her, lightened, and smiled.

All winter long he liked to build radios, take them apart, build them again. She loved to watch his long, square-tipped fingers selecting a part from the pile, turning it over, trying it out, reaching for a tool.

It made her proud that he found something he loved doing, that he wanted to be doing. She never tried to find out what he was thinking about—she wouldn't have intruded. Maybe, if somehow, she had—oh but she didn't know any better, how could she? You don't pick at another person's thoughts.

But he was her son, her child.

She wouldn't have thought he'd be one to drink. But when they found him shot on the riverbank twenty years ago, it was for worse than drink that he died. He was bootlegging liquor into dry villages. Someone drunk on the Calvert's that Paul planned to sell downriver shot him in the stomach, left him to bleed in the wet silt, the steep eroding bank above the river, among the willow roots. How could her son lie so still? And broken? Anabel knew death by then, knew it pretty well, but that Paul's face would never change with his thoughts again—that he would never live down this sin against them all, because if he had lived he would have lived it down, overcome this visit to hell, she knew it—Anabel could not believe the sudden hole in the world. The drop-off into the cold, sucking current of the river. There was no bottom to it.

She took her grief inside the cabin and sat down on Paul's bed and stayed there for three days, the grief sitting on her until she embraced it and lay with it and refused to move, held it in her arms like it was Paul himself turned to stone. When her husband tried to rouse her, she screamed and threatened him like a drunken woman. To have someone who should know better try to come between her and her grief! How she raged at him, tore at him! Anabel who never drank but once, with the redheaded soldier, and then only a taste, to keep him laughing with her. But still she wouldn't sleep with him. Only dance.

The hideous shadow fell: Paul's gone. She held that grief like a stone doll, though it threatened to eat her alive, she held it against herself, she lay with it as rigid and deep and hard as Paul's eyes that spring day, until finally it rolled away and she got up. And went about her business. Four children gone. Two sick when they were so tiny and helpless, died in her arms, and then Roy froze out here after a party, to no one's surprise, and then Paul.

And she'd mourn him again, from time to time, all of a sudden, wouldn't she? She just never got over Paul. Like this moment, here. If she could dance, she would, and if one person were to come and take her hand that she could choose out of all creation it would not be her husband, good kind tease that he used to be, it would not be the redheaded soldier, it would be Paul.

The mother from the family that just came in sat down next to Anabel with a cup of green beer and a shamrock cookie. She touched Anabel's shoulder in greeting and dipped her cookie in the beer. She was a plump young woman with curly brown hair. Her face looked like a face in paintings—heart shaped, perfect, framed by glossy curls. She had freckles and a quick, sweet smile. Somehow she gave off warmth. She brought a radiating heat into the room when she visited her sick mother. They usually came separately, the wife and the husband. Perhaps they were not getting along. Even now she ignored him. He sat a few chairs away, nodding to the residents on either side, helping a few of them get straightened in their chairs, or reach drinks that had wandered away.

But then he turned and watched the musicians, and there was wonder in his face. He looked stunned. *What am I doing here?* he seemed to be thinking.

Anabel could feel the mother's feet tapping, the faint vibration of her excitement.

"That's my cousin," Anabel told her. "The fiddle-player who sings, that's my cousin from Galena."

The mother peered and smiled and nodded. Green sprinkles clung to her lips. Her two youngest children were still circling the food table, drawing smiles. She kept her eye on them, frowned at the older boy who was still reading, and then shrugged at Anabel, as if to apologize for her boy's manners. Down the table the father had put a hand against the shoulder of the woman next to him, Alma, who had a tendency to slip helplessly to one side or another and needed to be shoved upright. The father shoved, Alma nodded and thanked him. He started talking to her.

The wife gave him a glance, an impatient sort of glance, as if to make sure he was behaving himself.

The musicians played a song Anabel hadn't heard in a long time. *Tra la la, tweedle dee dee, it gives me a thrill, to wake up in the morning to the mockin' bird's trill.* The melody took hold of her by the waist like there really was somebody reaching out to her, lifting her off her feet. Anabel, who weighed sixty pounds more than she did at twenty, suddenly was as light as a girl again, dipping from side to side like a stalk of grass. Her feet, both of them, itched to dance, and she tapped her toes on the dayroom floor, hoping to get someone's attention. Oh, good lord. She looked down where her skirt dropped off at the knee, dropped straight down, cloth hanging empty.

Son of a gun. Fill fruit jar and be gay-o.

Her husband, Archy, should have seen this. Anabel Hughes with one leg. Oh, he wasn't such a fine figure of a man himself. She missed him though, missed his heavy shoulders and his strong back and his small, wrinkled bottom that couldn't hold his Levi's up at all. So different from a woman. She missed the soft places at his waist where her hands could rest when she pecked him in the morning. She came back from Fairbanks after the first surgery on her knee ten years ago, and they had four days together before he got that tightness in his chest and that scared look just for a minute in his face. She missed him sitting in his brown plaid shirt watching her sew or watching the television, the two of them watching each other grow older.

She was too busy to mourn him properly. Too glad to have survived cancer and see her children and grandchildren again. So she didn't get the mourning taken care of. And then, to her surprise, she liked being alone, or having just her and her daughters in the house, not doing for a man, a bed to herself—it was a strange feeling, a refreshing feeling. So she never got to mourn him and maybe that's why it hurt again, from time to time. The warmth and heat of him. The difference of him. She got tired of the sight of her own self these days, that's the truth. Archy was easy to be with after thirty-seven years. When he died there was a novelty in being alone. Then she started to miss him, to miss what she would never have again, that warmth and heat, that bulk beside her, familiar but different, the demands he made by just living there, kept the place a little on the rough side, different that's all. Just different. Man and woman never do fit with each other like socks. They're going to be different, strange to each other, until the very last breath.

They walk heavy. Men thump into the house, make it shake. No need to, they just do it.

Tra la la, tweedle dee dee, there's peace and good will, Hudson sang. Anabel turned to the woman next to her. Somebody shouldn't waste Hudson's good music. In Galena, people wouldn't sit still like this.

"You should dance with your husband," she said.

"What's that?" the mother leaned in, as if she couldn't hear.

"You dance with your husband," Anabel repeated, her own leg still rocking, her heart yearning to go with the young woman—dip, float, get up, and move. Oh, and they didn't always have young men or old men, and that was fine too. Many times the girls danced with each other. That was almost as good. Holding hands, swaying, nothing to be afraid of. *Filé gumbo!*

They'd be breast to breast almost, laugh into each other's faces—oh, sometimes it was almost more fun with a girl!

"All right, then," said the mother and she stood up, stuck out her chest, and walked around the table to her husband. She stood there a moment, then she leaned over him and her red lips were smiling as she whispered. He consented.

There. That looked better. Here was a room with her cousin playing the fiddle and people dancing, a couple dancing. The spiritual son couldn't help but look up from his prophecy book, take a good look at Mom and Dad four-stepping. They had the floor to themselves and made the most of it. Sailing. Son of a gun. Watching her face, the father pushed her away from him a little tentatively, but she took him up on it, knew what he was offering her, and twirled. On the three count she was flung way out and with the next beat she was back in his arms. Not bad.

The thing about this cancer, it could come back. Maybe a little was left behind, even, waiting to start chewing on her again. This could be it. Eat up boys, this could be it, Archy used to say at breakfast time.

It was no way to go, a piece at a time. Pain and fear like wild dogs. Oh, God, where do these thoughts come from?

"First prize goes to couple number one," said Hudson into the microphone. Then he started another song. *Hey, sweet baby,* he sang, looking right at Anabel. *Don't you think maybe we could find us a brand-new recipe?*

Anabel fixed her gaze on his and sang back to him, softly to herself. *There's soda pop and the dancin's free.* Something about a wooden leg. Never mind the wild dogs, doctor said something about a wooden leg. Not wooden, anymore. Plastic and steel, could get one that gives when you press it, like a real leg. Like a real, strong leg, that is. The soldier's leg. Archy's. Now look at that cocksure fiddler up there, isn't he proud of himself and what would he think to see me dancing again, just a little bit, just a little bit of a waltz with my grandson. Dancing with Grandma and her artificial leg. Wouldn't he have a story to tell.

Rara Avis

When Holly Wiburg moved from Healy, Alaska, to Seattle in 1985 to attend library school, the gray, damp city drove her into herself. Not one good cold snap arrived to slap her awake. The contained wildness of Lake Union, at the foot of the campus, attracted and troubled her. She couldn't get out there, she couldn't lose herself in that freshness anymore.

Her height of almost six feet, her strength, her uncut red hair, things that made her stand out in Alaska, here in Seattle sent a different message: *Ignore me, I'm old-fashioned, I don't count.* Holly felt herself becoming invisible. If a tree falls in the forest when no one's around, does it make a sound; and if one library science student disappears, does anyone notice? What if I were to vanish into this crowd?

Then you wouldn't get your degree. Come on. You don't have to carve your initials in this place, you just have to show up every day.

When she was called upon in her classes, her own shyness appalled her. A woman who last year killed and butchered her third moose over the past three years—what if these people knew that? But here in these classrooms she would open her mouth and go into reverse. Don't listen to me, get me out of here, ran the subtext under her minimal sentences. The professors smiled. How they recognized it, or so they thought, this old-style reticence of the book-lover who decides to become a librarian.

But that first spring in Seattle changed everything. It came so early, and full bore—with songbirds, seed fluff in the air, the surprising spears of crocuses and snowdrops, and then suddenly cherry blossoms, dogwood, azaleas, and rhododendrons. Masses of bloom appeared against the shabby old houses, the concrete steps that led her onto the campus. The sky cleared up. Blue days raised the roof of the world. The lake water sparkled.

In her life she had never known a spring like this. The staff in Special Collections, where she worked part time, cranked the tall windows on ironwork frames open to the chestnut trees. Several times a day Holly leaned into the scented air and fell in love with this bright and temperate spring.

The architecture in her wing of the library enchanted her—the tall, tinted windows, the hardwood furniture and floors and wall paneling, and thousands of irreplaceable, old firsthand accounts of life in the Pacific Northwest, including the former territory of Alaska. Except for the Alaska Railroad hotel and a log cabin or two, few buildings in Healy, Alaska, were even thirty years old. In fact, much of Healy consisted of prefabricated metal units, hauled to Healy after they were abandoned by the oil companies in the late1970s. There wasn't much to look at in Healy, unless you looked up at the mountains.

After the pipeline boom in the '70s, Alaskans had money in the bank for the first time in their lives. In Holly's case it was the first time there was extra money in generations: her father, who owned a junkyard outside of Fairbanks, never had one spare dime. In 1969 when Holly started college, it seemed that everyone was living on the edge. Going to school, in those days, was a fairly cheap and comfortable way to live. But after college she went to work for Alyeska Pipeline Service Company and saved fourteen thousand dollars in three years.

She left it alone while she worked in Healy. She only knew how to live as a tightwad, and she would not have been able to spend that money on material things. In 1985 she was going to graduate school on it.

When Lucy, her supervisor, showed her around Special Collections, Holly recognized *Ogilvie's Survey of the Yukon Territory* stamped in gold on a heavy leather binding and reached out to remove the book by pulling it from the top of the spine. To her horror the edge of the old binding crumbled under her fingertips like a shortbread cookie. Her face flamed. Lucy reached back and removed the book properly by pushing in the volumes on either side, then carefully grasping the center of the spine. Holly thought, I want to go home. I don't know how to be here!

But spring changed all that. You couldn't breathe in that scented air without breathing in some courage, even if it was just the courage of impatience and longing.

The Rare Books librarian, Pamela, boasted her own library assistant, her personal slave, as Lucy often complained: Aggie Metheny. Holly never realized quite how lovely Aggie really was until she saw her against the backdrop of spring.

Stepping into Pamela's large office one day, she saw Aggie at the windows, arms outstretched as she pushed the panes out. Aggie's reddish brown curls shone like a river as they fell halfway down her back. She was slim and muscular, with a round behind in a short denim skirt, wine colored tights, leather boots. When Aggie turned, Holly looked away, embarrassed to be caught staring. Her gaze took in the front of Pamela's desk, with its handsomely lettered sign that said *Rara Avis*. At that instant Holly made up her mind: the assistant, Aggie, was the true rare bird.

"Hi there, Holly," said Aggie.

"Hi, Aggie. These books are for Pamela." Pamela Jones was a tall, thin, energetic librarian of maybe thirty-five, very professional, nasty, and sharp, with big breasts and red lips. Prematurely mature.

Somebody who really had put away her childish things and thrown away the key. But she must be doing something right, to have this lovely assistant on her team.

"Oh," said Aggie, "I'll take them. She needs them right away. Thanks." And she moved past Holly, scooped up the books, twirled past and out the door the way a branch whirls in fast water. Holly watched her go. "The Gam Queen," Lucy called Aggie, with blatant and affectionate envy, because of her colorful stockings and short skirts. Sometimes she wore lace stockings. And her legs were worth it.

Holly crossed the Rare Books office to look out the window as Aggie had done. The thrill of Aggie walking by her was so surprising, she wanted to revisit it, stay in it, this teasing mixture of confused desire and a voluntary, highly disciplined restraint at the same time. A strangely exciting surge of feeling, held in check. Where did all this come from? Did it come from missing Max, her boyfriend in Healy?

Somehow Holly didn't think so. It had nothing to do with Max. She thought of Max's chest and arms in his favorite worn flannel shirt. Thinking about him made her feel soft and reflective. Well, she did miss parts of him, sure, but not so much that she'd go crazy. In fact there had been times that she hated the physical way Max took on the world. The way, for instance, he used those long thin arms of his to throw off the blankets every morning and hurl himself into the day like an overdue Messiah.

There was nothing needed doing that he couldn't do, no problem he couldn't attack. At least he thought so. *If only he wouldn't be that way*, she thought, and smiled. *Don't be that way*, he used to say to her. What kind of request was that? Now she was thinking the same thing about him.

She leaned out the window into the breeze, the seed fluff drifting all one way, like notes on a page. Three stories below students went back and forth. How pleasant it was to be above them. It was a beautiful airy cage, this library. The library in Healy, where she worked for three years before coming here, was a double-wide trailer with metal shelves for books and kiosks of rubber-coated wire for paperbacks, videotapes, and magazines. You were constantly tripping over children's boots flung off just anywhere.

Even so, in that library she had felt, for the first time in her life, home at last and able to welcome others. That's why she was here. Everyone at the Alaska Library Conference told her you can do more for your library with the degree—you can fight for a budget. So Holly was after the degree, and here in Seattle she was disintegrating, her edges blurring. She was a heavy bird standing on the edge of the road, relying on camouflage. It usually worked, too. Get the degree and get the hell out.

Holly, don't be that way, don't use that language.

One morning the head of Special Collections, a distant, suited man named Randall—whom Holly had often seen reading to himself in the stacks and had carefully avoided, just as he seemed to be avoiding other people—collapsed walking down the steps from his front yard to his car in North Seattle. As it turned out, he barely survived an esophageal hemorrhage. Pamela Jones was appointed acting head of the collection.

The appointment of the rare bird to top management disturbed the other staff. Lucy muttered that under Pamela, order would be maintained even if Pamela herself were to crack up. Pamela would reassure the higher-ups that they were always in control.

The remarkable teamwork of the library staff was fractured by dissent. Desks were shifted, furniture rearranged, offices exchanged. Lucy made soft but caustic remarks about Pamela the full-breasted twit. Holly enjoyed Lucy's nastiness but did not think the remarks were always fair. Pamela couldn't help her display; it was God-given. Or could she? Could one preen too little, or too much?

I am definitely under-preening, she told herself, looking in the bathroom mirror. Didn't I used to have a waist? Muscles? Wasn't I the strongest girl at Lathrop High School in 1970? Didn't I cut some kind of outline against the crowd? Her first boyfriend, Duncan, thought so—he'd say exactly that. *Some kind of outline.* He'd say it adoringly.

For exercise, Holly herself walked everywhere. It was easier to walk across Seattle's neighborhoods than to stand at a bus stop in the cold.

She walked two miles every morning to the library from her rented house above Lake Union, and more often than not, she walked home again at night.

Most nights a busker would be entertaining pedestrians outside the used bookstore on Forty-fifth Avenue. It might be a singer with a guitar or a couple of bongo drummers, but Holly's favorite was the harmonica man—a shabby, dark man who never looked up. He played Stephen Foster songs, or Irish airs. She'd cross the street to walk past him and delight in the high, sweet music cutting through the hum of the city.

Holly lived on the first floor of a rundown house, on a whole street of rundown houses, and three Middle Eastern women climbed an outside set of stairs to the second floor. At night a vigorous tapping came from above, like a woodpecker. Weeks passed before she put the sound together with the smells that drifted down and realized that the women were chopping vegetables and spices for some wonderful ethnic dinner.

If she felt restless or claustrophobic on Sundays she would walk over to the zoo or down to Lake Union, fill her eyes with forms and colors and sounds you would never see in Alaska. Great diversity of flora and fauna was not a characteristic of the wilderness where Holly grew up; there were maybe five or six kinds of trees, six wildflowers she could think of now. Nor was there great diversity in Healy—no architecture to speak of, the school was a big box, the two churches were smaller boxes with pretty roofs, and the menu at the Sourdough Inn had been fixed for some time. Beef tips in gravy tasted the same year in and year out.

And yet, in a way, people in Seattle settled for less. Concrete everywhere and the monotonous roar of traffic from I-5. You couldn't get away from the roar, but this wasn't the Nenana River sounding in your ears. It was eight lanes of commuter traffic all day every day. It took something like the broken-down harmonica man to break into that dull background roar, to wake you up to something more like birdsong. To a tune inside.

How could people live like this, and wait in long lines for everything? Docile as the Christian girls in the church Holly used to go to, growing up in Fairbanks. Somehow, in college and after, docility had fallen away from Holly along with the companionship of the church. She got used to being on her own, but she did miss the companionship and that sense of purpose. You give up this, you get that. So what do the people in this big, wet, dazzling city get for living here, for putting up with all these fumes and crowds and the acres of concrete, the imprint of man everywhere you turn your eyes?

Oh don't be like that, she scolded herself. *They live this way because they like it. But I don't, much, though I sure do like the spring,* she thought.

Aggie Matheny stood up from her crouch between the stacks. Her eyes squeezed shut, her reddened cheeks wet with tears. She turned away from Holly.

"Aggie?" said Holly, and touched the sleeve of Aggie's blouse. "What's wrong?"

"Come here," said Aggie, and she walked out through the stacks, through the chain of offices to the staff bathroom. Inside she turned toward Holly with her hands to her face. It was clear that she expected to be taken into Holly's arms.

Holly opened her arms to gather up the smaller woman, and Aggie walked into her embrace and began to shake with sobs.

"What? What is it?" Holly said.

"All my friends are dying," said Aggie. "Why do all my friends have to die?"

"Who is dying?" said Holly, as gently as she could.

"Someone I really depend on, my friend Esther. Why are we all dying?"

Holly had been frightened by Aggie's tears; she almost felt relief, now that she understood what she was dealing with. This was understandable grief for one dear friend. Nobody's friends were all dying.

Aggie leaned into her completely and Holly held her close, one hand on Aggie's back, near her waist. She had never held a woman before, except for loose guarded hugs at church when she was in high school. Aggie's back muscles were rounded and smooth, shapely, not a broad scaffold like Max's. She quivered a little in Holly's arms like a wild animal.

Holly thought with amazement, *this is the first real hug of my life.* The palms of her hands were soaking up information while this young, trusting woman was wracked with grief, but she couldn't help herself. She wanted to move her hand down Aggie's ribcage to the small of her back, follow the curve of her waist.

Aggie's hanging on but I'm doing the hugging, she realized; it's up to me. She pressed Aggie's thick, silky hair. Then she pulled herself away in order to look the smaller woman in the face, and struggled to find words.

"Tell me," she said. "What's going on?"

"She had three years in remission. Now she's going to die. I've lost so many friends."

"Have you?"

"Oh, yes. Rocky, and Sage, and now Esther, just in the past couple years. Why does everyone I love have to *die*? No one knows how bad it is."

Holly gazed wonderingly down at her.

"I'm so sorry," she said at last.

"Oh, God," said Aggie. Then, "I'll be all right. I'd better wash my face. You go on ahead, I'd better clean up."

"Are you sure? Can I take care of anything?"

"No, thanks." Aggie sniffed, her face red and pulpy with crying.

"Why are your friends dying, Aggie?"

"I wish I knew."

"Take your time, okay?" Holly said at last. Her right palm tingled with a desire to return to Aggie's shoulder.

She went back to the book stacks, feeling both stunned and privileged, and gathered the books abandoned on the floor. They were all about Northwest Coast Indian art. Masks, bowls, scoops. The books were heavy, filled with colored plates. Pamela Jones was an expert in this type of thing. Aggie had been checking something for Pamela. *Aggie is too good for Pamela,* Holly thought sternly. *The world isn't right. It isn't fair.*

She put the heavy books on a nearby cart.

I don't even know her. I don't know what this feeling is. I don't want anything to do with a woman. Not me. I would rather be with Duncan again, or with Max. He can't help being so long and angular. He tries.

I could lose myself in Max, if I could just be what he wants me to be. If only that softness, that vulnerability, that came over him sometimes—after sex—stayed with him a bit longer. He put it aside immediately like he was ashamed of it. But it was so nice when he was like that, and we would lie there afterward feeling each other's breath, coming in and going out. So tender, that part. Exposure's not only in getting naked but in breathing against each other. Because you need each breath to stay alive, you're sharing your closeness to life, to death even, when you breathe together.

She liked waking up in the morning with her arm over Max, her knees bent into his, and his body so still, so available, so completely given up to being with her. Even if just because he was half asleep.

She had spent ten minutes leaning over this book on Northwest Coast masks and not seeing a thing, because her head, her memory, her fingertips, were full of thoughts of Max and Aggie.

"—a grant writer from the Burke Museum!" A sharp voice from the front of the room. "And I'm not ready!" Soft syllables from Lucy and the gunshots of Pamela's heels on the floor. Holly peered out of the stacks as they came toward her.

"Everything good we have on Northwest Coast art," Pamela was saying to Lucy.

"Maybe you're looking for these books," Holly said, pushing the cart up the aisle toward them.

"I suppose Aggie got called away?" Pamela said.

Pamela was in pain. Self-importance blinded her. It was a beam in her eye, a hard thing to tote around.

"I have it," said Pamela, seeming to accept that her question would not be answered. She reached and swiveled the cart away from Holly, expertly turned it, and began to maneuver it back to her office.

"Is that all you need?" asked Lucy.

"How do I know?" Pamela called back over her shoulder.

Lucy looked at Holly, shrugged and smiled. Her eyes crinkled into appealing slits when she smiled.

"Know where Aggie is?" asked Lucy.

"Taking a few minutes," said Holly.

Lucy sighed and sat down on a kick stool.

"Grant deadlines are upon us," she said. "Prepare yourself."

"For what?"

"Over half of our budget is grants," said Lucy. "There's no one as panicky as a grant writer behind schedule. Do you take grant writing in library school these days?"

"No. Public Library Management."

"It doesn't include grant writing? Go find a course and take it now. What's in Public Library Management?"

"Tell you the truth," said Holly, "that was last fall and I can't remember. Not much of anything."

They both laughed.

"The professor did say," Holly added, "that whatever is on the street will come into your library. If it's out there, it'll be in here."

"That's good enough, I reckon. Are you still thinking of going back to Alaska?"

Holly gazed down at Lucy on the kick stool, who leaned back to hug a raised knee. Lucy had the nicest way of stopping what she was doing, and relaxing with a patron, relaxing with Holly or another student worker. She took time to be with you.

But Lucy belonged here, like the robins in Holly's backyard early every morning. Lucy was a gentle and lovable temperate-climate forager with keen eyes and a sharp beak, well suited to this place. But she didn't understand this other thing, this need of Holly's for a double-wide trailer filled with paperbacks and battered videocassettes, the weather outside thirty below zero with the Healy wind howling, and no other cultural resource within one hundred miles.

"Where else could I possibly live?"

"You Alaskans," Lucy said. "The few I've met, you all talk so hopelessly in love with the place. I bet it's wonderful."

Holly wanted Lucy to understand her, but Lucy couldn't. Lucy was at home here. How can a person who is *home* understand what's going on inside a traveler who is lost and just putting in the time?

A wide hallway lined with card catalogs and computer stations led into Special Collections. Narrow tables ran down the middle. When Holly left that afternoon, the patrons should have been gone already, but one man still wearing his backpack sat at a table at the very edge of his chair, a temporary perch, as if he were on his way somewhere else. He was turning the pages of a book of photographs.

"Can I help you with anything?"

"I'm waiting for Aggie. I'm her husband."

At that Holly paused, she couldn't help it, to study him, and having accidentally displayed interest, was now forced into a conversation.

"This is my own book," he said. "I mean I checked it out from the main stacks. Is Aggie about ready, do you think?"

"I think so." She looked at the book. Audubon plates. "You're a bird man?"

"Raptors," he said.

Holly pulled out a chair and sat down, also on the edge. She had to look at him a minute longer, without being rude. He was matchstick thin, with straw-colored hair that stuck out and a very serious, sharp face. An incredibly drab mate for her Aggie.

"Are you the one from Alaska?" he said.

"Yes."

"I'd love to go up there. I looked into a postdoc at the university in Fairbanks. Though I'm not sure Aggie would do well there."

"Do well?"

"She's a dancer. She needs the city lights, the culture." He looked a little self-satisfied. Blaming Aggie for his own ambivalence. "Phil Saulter," he said.

"I'm Holly. Well, I like it up there. Raptors—that's hawks and eagles?"

"Birds of prey," he affirmed. Nonmigratory birds, she thought. Suddenly his pale blue eyes focused and sparkled: Aggie came out of the rare books office wearing her fringed brown suede jacket, ready to go home.

"Hi Holly. Hi Phil," she said and smiled wearily.

"Rough day?" he said.

She murmured, "I'll tell you about it later but Holly already knows; Esther's cancer is back in full force." Tears came into her eyes.

"Oh, Ag." He murmured sympathetically. But then he said, "It's such a high risk population."

"What do you mean?"

"I mean what you said before, your dancer friends are dropping like flies."

"Dropping like flies?" said Holly, astounded. *Flies?*

"There are a lot of gay people in the company. It's tragic but true. It's an endangered bunch of folks."

"Esther has cancer," Aggie corrected him.

"Well, there's something to it, there's something to what I'm saying. Too many of them are dying. I wish you'd get out of it."

"Oh, Phil," Aggie said, cocking her head at him. Holly was appalled at what he was saying—"I wish you'd get out of it" just like that? And what was she supposed to do with herself? But Aggie smiled faintly and looked somewhat restored. "I'll take my chances." She smiled at Holly.

Walking home, Holly tried to figure it out. Maybe Aggie was used to this guy. Something in his dryness and dullness calmed her down. She didn't want a mate to keep up with her on the dance floor, she wanted a reliable mate to cuddle up with at the end of a tough day. A guy who wasn't going to pull any surprises. Could that be it, the hidden connection more important than any obvious one? Maybe there's some kind of submerged instinct where you're really just choosing a father for your kids, not a personal mate at all, and you don't even know what you're looking for?

Holly and Max connected, they truly did, for a couple of years. But she didn't miss him enough, she could see that now. She couldn't imagine describing to Max the thoughts that went through her head as she worked so closely with Aggie, Pamela, and Lucy, the sights and sounds of Seattle.

Max worked at the Healy Coal Plant. He was a gifted, energetic engineer, with a real zest for the outdoors. But his eyes flattened when he did not understand her. That alone confused her, and made her want to stop talking. *"Holly, don't be that way."*

Holly had never had a close girlfriend; it just never worked out. She was a busy girl in high school, very much in demand at home. Girls struck her as silly. As a freshman in college, as her evangelical faith began to fall from her like excess layers of clothing on a warm day, she met Duncan, a musician and biker. Duncan accepted everything, her strange and difficult father, her spotty Christianity, her odd habits, her size and her shyness; and in Duncan's company she didn't need her familiar supports quite so much anymore. But Duncan was a free spirit. He begged her to travel with him; she had absolutely no desire to hop on the back of his Indian and see America over his shoulder.

It was a good day for her when she told him no. It was a way of defining herself. "I want to stay here," she said simply. "My future's here. I have things to do in Alaska."

"Make money?" he said gently.

She gave him a soft slap on the face in reprimand. "I'm a homebody, Dunc. I don't travel. I sink down, I stay put. I have things to do here."

"Your father doesn't need you anymore."

"It's not my father's needs I'm talking about." She was proud of having said that, of meaning it; she almost wanted to write it out big and put it up on the wall. Duncan was so good, in his own peculiar way; he stopped begging, and just loved her. It was hard to see him go. He sent her postcards for a year. Then, no doubt, he met someone else.

A few years later she met Max and put an end to loneliness. Someone who could keep up with her, outdoors or in! He was all in favor of library school; he seemed to think that the two of them had a plan. But during Christmas vacation last year she caught him looking at her from time to time as if he too had his doubts. There were long gaps in their conversations.

Pale yellow metal shelving rose above her like the walls of a mining tunnel, jammed with periodicals and boxes of microfilm. Holly was on her knees hunting for a quarterly when she nearly bumped into a fellow student—Lise, another older woman with life experience behind her. Lise checked her printed citation against the stacks and grabbed the journal she was looking for off the shelf.

"Working on your final project?" Holly said.

"Oh yes," Lise said, and smiled. She had loose, light brown hair that looked like it had just been sprung from French braids.

"What are you doing it on?"

"Cataloging Judaica," said Lise, and a flush of joy came to her cheeks. Holly sat back spellbound.

"Finding a lot?"

"Enough. How about you?"

"Lending networks between libraries," said Holly, embarrassed to have chosen such a dull topic.

Lise smiled. "Good luck," she said in the breathless voice of a woman aroused, and backtracked down the narrow space between the stacks.

Judaica. A word lovely enough to be a woman's name. And the happiness in Lise's face, in her skin—where did that come from? As if she was alive and hungry way down deep, where you were supposed to be. Holly sat back straight-legged and let the journal she was holding slide down her stomach. Oh, God, what is wrong with me? Oh, God, please help me because I don't know.

She came out of Werner's European Bakery a few days later with two almond wheels in a bag and saw Aggie coming toward her up University Avenue in a sharp April wind, a sheaf of flyers in her hand. Aggie smiled; the tip of her nose was red. Her gloves were thin and black, and a long, soft, red scarf circled her shoulders. Holly thought, could that be it? Am I in love?

She said, "Hey, what's the flyer?"

It was advertising an HIV-AIDS benefit concert.

"I'm thirty-two years old," she said to Aggie. "And yet I feel like a kid. I don't know anything. I know nothing of all this."

"You aren't the only one," said Aggie. "Don't feel bad. How could you know?"

"Can I help you put these up?"

"It's quick enough. But listen, if you're free, why don't you come? It's at the Last Exit on Brooklyn. The coffeehouse. You can sit with me. I'll save you a chair at my table." In her offer was a faint, all but hidden note of pleading. Almost as if she herself was scared to attend but if she could have Holly's company she'd do the brave thing. *Please sit with me.*

"Sure," said Holly.

"Great. Terrific. I'll be there about nine."

Of course, that couldn't be true. Aggie wasn't fainthearted; Holly was hearing things. Just the same, that note, whether real or imagined, went deep and pulled Holly in.

The Last Exit coffeehouse was big, crowded, and dimly lit. The walls were painted black, and a single candle stuck in a Chianti bottle decorated every table, along with skinny fliers listing AIDS statistics under the heading, SEATTLE CARES. On the stage were the confused shapes of amplifiers, a keyboard, several microphones. Holly forced herself to enter and walk among the tables, looking for Aggie. All these people in their twenties, aggressive and hip and experienced, intimidated her. I've tracked moose through bear country, she said to herself, I can do this. But are those two men really—are they kissing? Are all these people gay? Why do they do these dangerous things, these foolish things?

She saw several women with short, spiky hair, some with crew cuts! and thought, *not me.*

"Holly." Aggie was smiling, waving. The chair next to her was tipped forward so its back rested on the table. She was saving a seat just like she'd promised. Holly smiled, instantly relieved to see her. Phil sat to Aggie's right, and she didn't mind seeing him, either. On the table was a saucer of condoms. Each table had one, she could see. She picked up the strip of paper that read SEATTLE CARES and looked at the statistics. Over eight thousand dead in the United States. Twenty thousand cases. Every major city in the developed world, it said, is dealing with AIDS. Aggie leaned her shoulder against Holly's.

"You made it," she said. "I'm glad. I think you have to go up to the bar if you want something to drink. Phil?"

"Oh sure," he said. "Can I get you something, Holly? I'm getting us some tea, why don't I order you something?"

"You don't have to."

"Not a problem."

She asked for coffee and milk, and as soon as Phil left, spread the little flyer on the tablecloth between Aggie and herself. She was suddenly outrageously happy. The strangeness of the surroundings mixed with the rightness of being next to Aggie. It was perfect. She was even comfortable admitting to Aggie that she had barely been aware of AIDS until recently.

"Few people are. But this is a start. Too late for a lot of people." Aggie took a deep breath, almost a gasp, as if at a private memory. "People have just disappeared. It's been so silent. You know what? President Reagan hasn't ever even mentioned the word in public! Phil can't get over that. To ignore the scientific interest of a new virus alone, let alone that it's killed thousands of people, for him not to mention it!"

A young man began to speak on stage, into a microphone. Though his voice was soft, it hushed the audience. He quoted the statistics on the flyer, and then said, "We're getting close to an antibody test. We need to remember, always, and tell everyone you know to remember this—that the incubation of the virus can be from five to ten years, or longer. Thousands of us still do not know if we are carriers. Think about that." He was thin and delicate, nearly bald, but even from where she sat Holly thought he had once been a redhead. Something about his skin, his eyelashes. "Remember," he pleaded with his audience, "when you and your partner get together, the other people you've been with even once over the past ten years—those people are having sex with you too!"

There were murmurs from the crowd, some clapping, a few outcries.

"And what if they keep a list?" one shouted. The audience wasn't completely friendly.

"Think of birds," said the young man on the stage. "This disease showed up in a vulnerable population, just like DDT showed up in the birds. When American society has a silent spring, will they notice us then? Will they think of us then, and wonder what is missing from their lives?"

Scattered, then stronger applause. Some shouted, "Where's the press these days?"

Will they wonder what is missing, she thought.

He introduced the band at last, to cheers, and five women piled onto the platform. The lead singer wore a sleeveless shirt with thin straps. Her neck, shoulders, and arms were pink and firm, her hair cut and combed into short, colorful spikes. She seized the microphone with confidence and began to joke with the crowd. "We're gonna restrain ourselves tonight, keep it simple," she announced, and the cheers increased. Everyone seemed to know her. A very big young woman sat behind a drum set and the music took off. For Holly's taste the sound was right up close to plain loud noise, but she found the lead singer's appearance and energy irresistible. This was some kind of blend of rock music and folk music, not homogenized but woven together. Elements of each stuck out: a beautiful refrain, a noisy crash of drums and chorus, a feeling that you wanted to be part of this wave of energy.

After an hour of music and then a couple of encores, the evening was over. People emptied the saucers of condoms on their tables, stuffed them into pockets as they left the coffeehouse. Phil lifted one. "Cinnamon," he announced.

The three of them left together and discovered they were all on foot. Phil and Aggie needed to walk over to University Bridge to get to their apartment on Capitol Hill; Holly accompanied them for five blocks. *We're an odd threesome,* she thought. She and Phil were like two cutouts framing this one, bright, warm light.

All my friends are Christians, she told Duncan, years ago, before it changed, before Duncan himself became her best friend. She thought she was tough, but she had been looking for safety: I only hang out with Christians. Why did she ever think that was a good idea? It was a lifelong habit. Choose carefully, stay away from people who don't understand you. And that's most people. Are all of us, the people among whom she grew up, fortified in their remote towns...are we just fearful people?

The three of them reached University Bridge. They stared at each other and then Aggie reached out and gave Holly a hug. Holly saw it coming, and hugged her back. Phil reached forward after a minute and gave Holly a dry peck on the cheek—whatever for? And yet she knew why, and patted his arm. It's because we're facing something and we don't know what to make of it, or what to do next. She looked at his light blue eyes and smiled. When he smiled back, though he had Aggie on his arm, he seemed to concede something to Holly.

It was some kind of recognition. Or respect. Maybe he liked people who liked Aggie. *You're all right.*

"Well, see you then, it was fun," she said. "That doesn't seem like the right word, but fun, and other things, you know."

"Goodnight, goodnight," they called, heading out on the bridge, over the neck of water between Lake Union and Portage Bay.

An untrimmed rhododendron dropped pink and brown blossoms at the edge of the sidewalk. These houses were neglected, the U. District was a virtual student slum, but no one objected. Tenants weren't here long enough to object. These streets were staging fields, no more. You had to walk farther away to see where people really lived.

She had been to Seattle only once before, at age ten when her mother died. She came to stay with an aunt for a week. It was wonderful. She didn't realize until twenty years later—after her father died—that the grownups had been wondering if she should move to Seattle, live with her aunt instead of that difficult, crazy, redheaded widower with the popping veins in his forehead and those opinions he had to make public every chance he got. Tears came into her eyes. *You wanted me back, Daddy,* she thought, *you argued to get me back to Alaska, to live with you. And I never knew. I wish there was someone with me now, so I could say, look at these flowers. Look at this city.*

Oh, I wish there was someone.

Aggie and Phil and Lucy didn't know anything about Holly's father, about Max, they didn't know her in connection to others; they looked at Holly and saw a woman alone. I have a little more freedom than either one of them—no one's clinging to me. I can be the one to decide how to go at things, make things happen back home. Not make Daddy's mistake, thinking I can do it all myself.

I can't do it all myself. But I am alone. I am more alone now than I have ever been.

See it through, Max used to say when things were tough, when they were panting up a slope, loaded down with packs full of game meat, miles from the truck. See it through. Tonight she didn't like Max very much, but his words were useful just the same.

As she headed toward the bright lights of Forty-fifth Avenue, two men sauntered down the hill toward her.

"Spare a buck for a cup of coffee?" asked one as they passed her—a small, hairy man in an army jacket.

"I don't have it," she said, as she always did, shaking her head.

"'T's okay, you have a good night, sister," he said, waved, and they walked on by.

Holly smiled, warmed inside. She turned west on Forty-fifth and moved along with the passersby. She looked at the globe in the window of the travel bookshop, another window filled with glittering drums and guitars, the Blue Moon tavern. Up ahead the all-night used bookstore with the harmonica man outside, an open case near his feet for spare change. He played several sizes of harmonica; they'd be fanned out in that case at his feet.

No one's let me down, she thought. It's not that. It's more that it's my turn now to walk through this alone-space. I have to walk through this space knowing that at the beginning and the end of it, and every day in between, I'm still sister to people I don't know. Here comes somebody's sister.

Her fingers dug at the seam inside her pocket and closed around several quarters. She liked to keep them handy for bus fare. But in fact, she never minded the miles—in fact, not one time had she regretted a single step of the long walk home. Any more than she'd mind the long flight back to Alaska, once she finished up here come fall.

Star of the Sea

1996

On one of her many visits to Seattle during the last year of their mother's life, Joy's sister, Alma, helped Joy choose a new pair of dress boots, made of waterproof leather, with high narrow ankles—perfect elegance for Seattle. Or Ireland, for that matter, if Joy ever went on a retreat to their ancestral homeland, which Alma recommended.

Alma went to Ireland to visit a Benedictine Abbey, but along with religious mysticism, she cultivated a fashion sense. Joy liked the boots, and she liked the emphatic sound they made on the uneven concrete floor of their mother's basement. Joy waved her arm in the air for the string from the light bulb. The string hit her fingers like the hem of a ghost and she gave it a yank. The basement came into view: its dark recesses of storage space, whitewashed posts, the low ceiling. How frightened she and Alma and Ty had been of this unfinished basement as children. How could their mother, their bold single mother, a fearless woman so impatient with human frailty have raised such timid, conservative children. The three McCracken kids wanted nothing more than to come home every afternoon from Our Lady Star of the Sea School to a casserole and Jell-O, a mom surrounded by bushels of fresh white laundry, a dishwasher humming, maybe the Mixmaster whipping up a chocolate cake. "Lick this," their dream mother would say, handing down a beater covered with chocolate batter. Such a thing had never happened.

Widowed at thirty-three, when her husband and infant daughter had been killed in an automobile crash on the way home from a well-baby checkup, Joy's mother had almost let the grief win. She was wild, absent, hollow-eyed. Then one night she came home sopping wet from visiting the cemetery during a rainstorm. Joy was shocked to see her mother standing there in the living room, in stocking feet, black hair plastered to her scalp. Helen McCracken was looking at a bramble that had inserted itself under the painted window sash and had started climbing the bedroom wall, thorns and all. It seemed as if things couldn't get worse; but suddenly Helen turned and looked at her oldest daughter and said, "Joy. That's that. I'm not going out there again. Despair is a sin. Did you have supper?"

Helen McCracken found herself the sole support of her family, and she decided to accept the job, as a veteran character actor would accept his assignment. There was now something she had to do, ten hours a day. Sometimes twenty-four. There would be moral satisfaction. There would be pleasure in it, eventually. There would be escape. It wasn't long before she joined the faculty at the University of Washington Department of Chemistry, and she never once suggested, after that day, that she might have chosen a different life if her husband and baby daughter had lived. She didn't talk about it: she spoke in a loving, friendly, teasing way about her husband, as if his absence was temporary, as if he were merely at work. She didn't talk at all about Barbara McCracken, aged six months.

Joy, Alma, and Ty grew up on the other side of a No Man's Land from the accident. Somehow they picked their way through the aftermath and landed together in a new country where they weren't in shock anymore, weren't weeping anymore. No one wanted to go back.

Yet there were ghosts. What is death to little children, especially if no one speaks of it? Some kind of robber, a successful one who got away. The basement, especially, was inhabited by ghosts—it was there that unresolved terrors lurked, that robbers crept inside and hid until your guard was down.

Their house, the house in which Helen lived until she died, was a shabby but comfortable bungalow near the University of Washington. During the Seattle real estate boom, Joy and Alma discovered that the little house on Hamlin Street might bring them and their brother several hundred thousand dollars. Joy's answering machine filled with queries and proposals from realtors. It was up to her to do the legwork: Alma lived in New Mexico with her third husband, and Ty lived east of the mountains, growing organic apples in the Yakima Valley. They would come to Seattle and walk through the house and sit helplessly with Joy afterward, make one suggestion or two (let's get a landscape guy to look after those roses) and then flee. Joy was appalled, later, at how little they had done, how much still remained to be accomplished, one decision at a time.

And yet Helen had done her part, in the last few years of her life. The whole house, actually, was far neater than it had ever been; in her last years Helen had gone crazy for neatness. She had been getting rid of things, storing things. If Joy left cooking ingredients after a party, they'd be waiting later in a neat row on the polished tile counter.

"Please take this baking powder home with you," Helen would say. "Isn't it yours?"

Joy always felt so puzzled, almost rejected by that behavior. Eventually she'd take home the baking powder, or cloves, or hoisin sauce, since otherwise it would stay there on the spic-and-span counter, waiting, a distress to her mother. On the gleaming tile, day after day, one unsightly can of Clabber's.

As she stood in the basement, lit by the single bulb overhead, she saw that Helen had not neglected the hidden recesses of the house. The basement too had been cleaned and organized. Helen had hired housecleaners and sent them downstairs. The floor was scrubbed and the plywood storage shelves filled with huge, stuffed plastic sacks, necks strangled with wire ties. There were boxes and footlockers under the shelves. Joy nudged one with her boot. A faded green footlocker. She bent and hauled it out from under the shelf. She looked at it with mild excitement, as if taking part in a scene from a gothic novel. There was a little padlock in the hasp, but a key dangled on a string. Always well organized, that was Helen.

Joy squatted on her heels in front of the trunk and fit the key into the lock. She lifted the lid.

So here's where they were.

The trunk was full of souvenirs from Washington beaches, things that Helen had collected over twenty years of summer vacations. Driftwood, shells, sea stars, bones. Joy had been wondering where the clutter of her mother's hobbies and passions had disappeared. Here it was, much of it, a beachcomber's treasures. Scientific projects that she never completed. Joy sensed her mother alone in the house quietly filling this trunk—why?—and was appalled. Surely lifting and storing each piece where she would never see it again—did she know that?—must have hurt. What compelled her?

These things—these were all treasures brought back from family vacations at the rented beach house on Hood Canal. Joy lifted out a yellow sea star. Her mom used to salt these things. They'd be lined up on the sea wall at the beach house, drying in the sun. Joy remembered the vivid differences in color from one starfish to another—orange, mustard, a deep rich purple. That was how they all were in those days—greedy. Taking things home, adding souvenirs to the hoard. Even though what Helen liked best about the sea star was that it could grow a new arm if one was severed. It would have to be alive to do that.

Joy set the star back in the trunk and lifted out a dish-shaped bone of some wild animal. Helen was always collecting such things. Once the skeleton of a bear.

What a day that was.

And here was a Japanese glass float! Why store this in a trunk? In the old days these floats, unbroken glass balls nestled in the limbs of a driftlog, perhaps, were worth their weight in—something valuable, if not gold. This one still had fishnet wrapped around it. From some fishing boat far out at sea to the beach at Tekiu Point or Cape Alava, it had arrived unbroken thanks to these thick strands of cushioning net.

The frayed net reminded Joy of something. What could it be? Ah, yes. Her little sister's braids—Alma's long, tight French braids, left for a few days, would be all rubbed and frayed like this net. Alma's braids on a camping trip, on a vacation.

1956

Helen McCracken had little use for religion. She would not take out a rosary during a gale like this one tonight. Instead she checked the batteries in the flashlights. She relished getting ready. She liked a storm!

At eleven Joy took for granted that her mother knew what was coming. Helen McCracken knew the gamut of calamities, would see them through. The rented beach house groaned in strange ways when the wind raced off the open water of Hood Canal and shook the house and the trees. Waves crashed into the sea wall, broken crests flung above the wall like hands waving for help. But her mother reminded them that the trees, the Douglas firs and the cedars, were well away from the house. Her mother never said things like, "It's all right, nothing can happen, I'm here." Instead she would say, conversationally, "I'm glad they cleared around the house. That's smart. In 1926, in Miami, no one had any idea."

"Tell us a story about the hurricane, Mom," said Joy's little sister, Alma, whose imagination ran to wild, lurid scenes. She looked up at mother the way you'd stare at a light on shore if you were crossing Hood Canal in the dark, in the rain. Eight years old, Alma focused hard on her own salvation. Stories were part of it. Joy sometimes resented the fact that Alma knew her own self so well. Strange feelings, envy and a little spite, a desire to punch Alma, moved in Joy sometimes and shamed her. Alma was so cute, so spoiled, so helpless really, but she had this unexpected ability to focus.

By contrast Joy sometimes felt like a mess. This storm on top of what happened yesterday. Getting her period. Maybe she'd feel cozier if she didn't have this thing between her legs now, have to get up and change it, and go through that whole business in the dark bathroom with a flashlight! Twisting that strap through the buckle with the flashlight gripped under one arm. Life could be terrible. Alma had no idea.

"I was ten years old and I was thrilled," said Helen. "The roof came right off our house. Lifted right off. They found ships on dry land, way farther inland. Of course I couldn't see the terrible destruction. It ruined my parents financially, they lost their stake, everything they came to Miami for. I couldn't see any of that, the terrible loss of property. I was just so excited!"

She talked as if any ten-year-old would be excited in a storm, but her own children were not thrilled tonight. Alma was scared and Joy was nervous. Ty wore his characteristic grimace of anxiety, as if he wasn't sure what was expected of him, the man of the house at six years old. He leaned against Grandma on the couch, his face pinched, hers serene. Joy's grandma, her father's mother, was saying a Rosary, but Gram always said the Rosary. Every day maybe. Gram loved praying to Mary, it was like they were friends having a conversation. Gram knew something about Mary that Joy did not, and never would. Joy wasn't even tempted to get to know Mary. Hail Marys were synonymous with penance. You're getting off easy once again. The pleasure of five Hail Marys.

She hadn't even gone to confession this year. She had just stopped going up with Helen to Our Lady every Saturday, and Helen didn't argue with her. "I lied, stole, and disobeyed my mother," Joy blurted out to Father Cox last year.

"Whoa whoa whoa," he said, and laughed. He laughed at her! She found it impossible after that to confess a real shame. She had made it up about the lying and stealing. She said her Hail Marys rapidly, especially that line about the hour of our death. Couldn't Mary set that hour back? Mary was cold and strange to Joy, almost mechanical, like all saints. Never a mess. When it was time to make a decision, saints always made the right one. They couldn't wait for the hour of their death.

But Joy still felt comforted by the sound of Gram's murmur, her serene reliance upon the Rosary, and she knew that Gram's presence was also a comfort to Helen. Gram brought familiar connections with her when she visited the McCrackens. She had never been to the beach house before. It was a huge house, built ages ago for a large family, and now rented out to summer visitors for weeks at a stretch. Joy could pretend it was their own family's house. Our summer house, she could say to herself.

A branch broke in the wind and hit the wall of the house. Gram's soft voice went right on through the Sorrowful Mysteries. Joy's mother never said the Rosary. But she seemed at ease being around someone who did. What did she think of Mary?

Would Mary really help you out in a storm? Or did she just give you the patience to suffer things that happened? Joy suspected the latter. Gram wasn't really asking for help. She was just having this conversation with Mary. But it did calm Alma down, at least, Gram's Rosary and mother's story about the 1926 hurricane. Joy had heard the hurricane stories before. What puzzled her and made her a little sad was that she and Alma did not seem to like storms as much as her mother did. A torrent of rain beat against the living room windows. This will never end, Joy thought. I'll never get to sleep. This is the worst night of my life.

But then she was waking up to yellow light behind the parted curtains. The storm was over, and so were her troubled dreams. She was filled with gratitude. The daylight was as beautiful as breakfast, as beautiful as gold. The storm was over, and the dream was no longer something she had to deal with. Burglars broke into the house, and one of them poised his big, ugly fist over her face. Joy closed her eyes and waited for the blow. She knew it would break her nose. It would smash her nose and hurt terribly. She squeezed her eyes shut and waited, knowing that somehow Alma was safe; she could take the blow instead of Alma, at least for the time being.

Because Joy did not cry out, the burglar was impressed. He let her go. I have to go to the bathroom, she told him. She crept away, down carpeted stairs, past a guard in the living room who was oddly reading a book—and out the front door conveniently ajar—and then up the street in search of help, running. She must save Alma. But all these houses were empty. For sale! No one lived on this street anymore! It was their street in Seattle, but all the neighbors had moved away. Why didn't Joy's family go with them?

At the top of the street she found a house where people were sleeping. Oh thank God. Parents had to be nearby. Now, she would call for help. Even though Joy knew there was a good chance the robbers had been here before. There was a good chance the sleeping forms around her might already be dead. Battered to death.

Her roars for help woke her up.

There was the yellow light outside the window. Alma in her sleeping bag next to the couch. Alma's loose brown braids, hairs escaping. Gram would rebraid that hair with a wet comb after breakfast. Alma's arms reached up out of her bag as if for rescue; she was too hot in her sleep. She had worn a sweater to bed. Voices, Mom and Gram, from the kitchen; a clatter. A cupboard door. A bit of strain in the voices. They were having a difference of opinion. Gram's voice was insistent, Mom's almost petulant.

Joy thought about her dream with amazement. Why wasn't I terrified, she wondered?

The kitchen door swung open. Mom appeared, her favorite coffee cup—the big red cap to a thermos bottle—in her hand and a certain expression on her face. Tight, needing to get away from Gram.

To get away. On the escape. Heading down to the beach.

After a storm, the pounded rocks would be layered and clean. Maybe a few surprises had washed up overnight, Helen said. Joy pushed out of her sleeping bag and stepped on Alma, who grunted and rolled over.

After breakfast—eggs scrambled by Gram, who wasn't saying directly what the quarrel was about but who dished up overcooked eggs and toast in far too great a quantity for Joy's taste—Joy and Alma made their own escape. They ran like sprung seagulls toward their mother's silhouette; she was far down the beach, bent over collecting oysters.

Hood Canal, a serpentine arm of Puget Sound, was not built up with summer houses at this end. Their own was one of the few within five miles of the village of Holly, with its pier and charter boats and ice cream cones. Between Holly to the north and their house on Tekiu Point, woods came down to the beach, dense cedar forests that seemed ominous to Joy. But the beach this morning was just as she had imagined. The flat, hand-size rocks had been lifted all night by the tide and the waves and allowed to fall back where they fit best. Sifted, in place, they were clean and pale and decorated with long streamers of seaweed. Helen walked at the water's edge, where it moved back and forth as gently as lace on a sleeve or a collar. When Joy caught up with her, she could see that Helen's face, like the beach, was smoothed of worry. All the tension was gone.

She has her beach face on, thought Joy.

Helen's canvas bucket was filling up with oysters, and she was eating oysters now. With a twist of her knife she opened one for Alma, who liked to keep up with Mom, do whatever Mom did; it was part of the bargain between them, Joy sensed. Do what Mom does and be guaranteed safety. Joy felt excluded, confused, by this. To make matters worse, Alma liked oysters. She sucked them down with a grin, her little throat working like a snake swallowing a mouse. She and Helen took such delight in themselves over their oyster-eating. Joy herself preferred scrambled eggs above all other foods, usually. Not as dry and in as huge a supply as Gram had foisted on her this morning, though.

"When I come here I like to eat oysters," Helen was saying. "I wish Gram would try them. She just wants to make scrambled eggs and pork roast and stew, as if we were back home in Seattle! Just like my own mother, for goodness sake!" She groused, but she was happy. The mysterious affliction of anger and sadness that sometimes had her in a grip had evaporated. They had been at the beach house for three days, and this was the happiest Joy had seen her mother.

Joy looked out at the wide, gray-blue canal, the blue ridge on the eastern side, the gulls circling, and felt happy too.

"She wants to go to Mass tonight," added Helen, in a quieter voice. It was Thursday.

"Why, Mom?"

Joy could feel her mother thinking, for a few seconds. She could sense that against-the-wall feeling looming close in the woman next to her. But it didn't take over.

"Well honey, it's your father's birthday."

A wave of guilt that she had forced her mother to say that. That she hadn't remembered. That she hadn't been ready.

"Why don't we do something," said Joy after a minute, swinging on a pendulum and longing to swing in the right direction.

"I don't really want to keep doing things like that," Helen said finally. "This is our vacation. We'll go to Mass on Sunday. Your father and I, we did other things. It won't bring him back. Gram said, he was my son. I said he was *my* husband. Perhaps I shouldn't have."

She walked down the beach, picking up oysters.

"Despair is a sin," she said. "I really believe that." She spoke with conviction, even satisfaction. "I learned that after he died."

It was not on the list of sins Joy was told to hold against her conscience before confession at Our Lady Star of the Sea. The nuns were clear on the procedure, how to find sins to confess even when none weighed heavily on your mind. Go over the Ten Commandments. No one said anything about despair. This one felt like Helen's own discovery. And the sin part was important. In the sin part, Joy was to realize many years later, lay her mother's salvation, her mother's comeback.

To fill the bucket, they had to wander a bit. They were maybe a mile from the house when they found the bear.

He was bigger than any of them. Humped on the beach. A skeleton, or most of one. Ribs and shoulder bones facing the beach. Some leg bones still attached, though barely. He hadn't survived the storm intact. Despite all the pounding and washing and scouring, he still stank once Helen, in wonder and curiosity, started touching the black gristle between his bones with the blade of her oyster knife. It was the gristle that stank. But it wasn't the worst smell in the world, just strong. They walked around him in amazement.

It wasn't long before Joy realized that Helen was infatuated. She took her knife and sawed a bit at where the scapula connected to the vertebrae, and she succeeded in separating them. She scraped at the scapula until the most of the gristle was gone and rinsed it over and over in the water of Hood Canal, scraping with her oyster knife and rinsing again, till it was almost clean. She held it up, looking at it. Joy was impressed: it was pretty and graceful, like a china dish.

"Can you imagine," she kept saying.

But it still smelled, like the other smell that bothered Joy. The smell when she changed her pad. She knew by now that smells lived in your head when there was really no cause for them. Once she smelled herself all afternoon, but when she checked, there was no problem, no mess. An intense and private smell in her head that no one else even knew about.

Before Alma and Joy knew what was happening, their mother was hauling them back down to the house, the pungent scapula in one hand and the bucket of oysters in the other, her eyes gleaming with purpose and desire.

It was as if Gram's worst fears were coming true. Helen was going to make oyster stew for supper, when she got around to it, and before that she was going to take apart, scrape clean, and pack home the skeleton of a black bear. Gram shook her head fiercely, her lips set, but she had to allow it. There was no stopping Helen, who was now full of talk about how a crock of dilute peroxide would clean them up, get rid of the smell—

"A good pickle crock!" said Gram.

"Mother," said Helen, "I've had those crocks for ten years. And I haven't made pickles yet. But this is something else! Please, I insist you come out and see it, sitting there, looking at the water."

While she was talking like this, trying to persuade, she was filling a Trapper Nelson, their father's backpack, with paper bags to carry home the bones. She opened a drawer and chose knives—a fish knife in a leather holster, a Boy Scout knife.

Joy liked it when Helen called Gram "Mother." She liked the reminder that no argument could change their fundamental relationship. Love lay underneath the argument like a hidden firmament.

Gram's problem was, she didn't know how to think about a bear. She didn't know how to think about finding a treasure on the beach. She had spent her whole life in Chicago and Seattle, organizing a household. She didn't know how to organize the retrieval of a bear skeleton. But Helen gave her a hint. Helen was a scientist. She had to do these unusual things, follow these scientific impulses. She had to explore the inner structure of things.

—

It took hours; Joy helped. They sawed at the joints and scraped the ends of the bones with tiny hard scrapes to get rid of the gristle. "Be careful always to move the knife away from your own body," said Helen. Gram sat down on a drift log, a long, wide, bleached column of fir that had got away from a log boom ages ago, and watched for a while. Before she made her way slowly back, she admired the bones as they went, scraped and salty, into paper bags. It was funny that she was wearing a skirt, Joy thought, but it would have been even odder to see her in pants. To see her in a man's wool trousers and fishing jacket, the way Mom was dressed. Gram was seventy-one. She had hair like Alma's, long and still brown, braided and curled on top of her head.

Joy was glad that her grandmother was reconciled to events. Happier still that Helen's stretch of enthusiasm had not worn off, that it would not, in fact, that the vacation lay before them like a sunny ridgetop. They had made it this far together. It really didn't matter anymore exactly how things turned out, because it was all treasures on a beach now. Beachcombers. With a big house to cozy up in at night, to feel rich in; it didn't matter that the house didn't belong to them, it was better that way, because they didn't have to take care of it—an invisible fleet of owners kept the sea wall up, the firewood chopped, the oak floors polished, the trees away from the house.

Ty loved dismantling the skeleton. When he tired of the work, he sailed skipping stones into the water. He would never leave the beach on his own. After they walked back with the heavy pack, Helen set the bones out to bleach on the sea wall, admiring each one and laughing at herself. The day we found the bear.

1996

Alma at forty-eight still had a striking beauty. At the wake, she was self-possessed; but later after most of the guests had gone, she leaned against Joy on the couch and cried. In the midst of her tears, a tiny endearing yawn escaped her. They were both so exhausted. Her hair had its customary too-long-between-haircuts look. Inside a soft camel blazer she felt all bones to Joy. Her three children had gone home with their father, Alma's ex-husband.

After a while Joy said, in wonder and confusion and sympathy as she felt tears on her own face, "I'm fifty-two, and I still want my mother."

"She knew what was coming," Alma said. "Getting rid of everything in the house, the way she did. I thought she was trying to keep the world's neatest house in retirement, that cleanliness was next to godliness, or at least next to a chemistry lab."

"She did know. The opposite of nest building. Something in her, was getting ready," said Joy.

"She always gave herself permission to do whatever she felt like," said Alma. "How did she manage to trust herself? I've never really understood that confidence."

Like her mother, as it turned out, Joy had always worked her way through calamity. Inaction felt like shame. Methodically, often without relish, she shoved on. But Alma—it seemed Alma embraced calamity, made despair into her twin sister. Her life would come apart at intervals. These days Alma spent a few weeks every year at a Benedictine monastery in Ireland—it seemed to help. Joy didn't know if it was the return to religion or something else that helped Alma pull herself together—solitude, or meditation. Long walks and simple food. Or were the frequent retreats another instance of Alma following her own behavior? She had always seemed to give herself lots of permission to do whatever she wished. But she suffered from her decisions afterward. She was a long time recovering.

Joy admired Alma's spirit. But she never knew quite what to say to her much-married little sister. It was easy to wound her.

"Despair is a sin," said Joy, and the two of them laughed at the familiarity of it. Their mother had certainly ignored her faith, most of the time. She let so much go by the way. But not the sin part; she needed that. That part of her legacy worked for her. *Mom, what have I inherited from you and my grandparents,* Joy wondered, *beyond a house that's wildly inflated in value, and a feeling for starfish and bones? What am I leaving my own children?*

She saw her mother again in the hospital bed. Bones. White skin. The soft murmur of the oxygen machine. The tube they tried repeatedly to force into Helen's nostrils—the nurses pushed, Helen screamed. They tried again and again. When they finally withdrew it they saw it had doubled up on itself, was covered in blood. Joy stood at the foot of the bed unable to move.

At the end death came like a friend they'd been waiting for. The oxygen machine and the blue stain of morphine brought comfort like the tide itself. Joy thought that she loved oxygen and morphine; she felt so grateful for the peace they brought to the room. The last few days were so quiet, even while they all waited on the edge. When she lifted the bedclothes to take her mother's hand, the skeletal, dehydrating body horrified her, but only momentarily.

One morning in the hospital, Joy and Alma and Alma's oldest son, Keenan, nineteen, drinking coffee in Helen's room, watched the sun rise over the Cascade Mountains. The walls of the room glowed as the streets below began to fill with commuter traffic. A bright, chunky woman suddenly whirled into the room like a little tornado.

"I'm Sister Marietta," she announced. "How are you today?" She shook hands with everyone and bent tenderly toward Helen. "Hello, dear. Would you like me to bless you? We sisters can do that now." Helen seemed to smile and beam, if only reflecting the sister's radiance. Sister Marietta took Helen's hand, made the sign of the cross on her brow, kissed her, and in a familiar singsong asked for God's blessing on this woman, your servant. She smoothed Helen's hair, promised to return, and almost as suddenly as she had come, whirled away.

"What was that?" said Joy, as the three looked at each other in mild and amused astonishment.

"I'm afraid I'm responsible," said Keenan, shaking his head.

"What do you mean, honey?" said Alma.

"Well this guy came in here earlier, this chaplain, when I was here alone, and he said would you like me to get a priest. And I said, meaning you two, I said well I think the sisters should handle that. And he said, Okay, I'll send in a sister."

When Joy laughed, her face hurt. She laughed and rubbed her face as if to rub the stiff muscles into compliance. Keenan's red hair and tall, angular body were full in the path of the sunrise. Alma gazed at him in delight.

"Let's say the Hail Mary," said Joy, and there was nothing to do but watch their mother as they said it, and say it about her. Blessed art thou, amongst women. Our mother of many arms.

As she crouched over the trunk filled with shells, driftwood, the combings of a lifetime of vacations on Pacific beaches, Joy couldn't shake the feeling of horror for her mother's isolation at the end. Why hadn't Helen passed these things out to the girls, or left them to decay outside? They don't belong here in darkness, they should be outdoors in the weather.

She dragged the trunk to the center of the basement floor, directly under the hanging bulb. Oh, Mom, I don't know if I can take any more surprises. Is there anything else? Or is that despair talking?

The sea oh the sea, bright love of my heart. One of Mom's and Alma's favorite songs. Mom, looks like you've left me one more thing to do. I think I will return these stars to the beach. This worm-eaten driftwood Keenan can stick pens and pencils in, on his desk in his dorm room. Someone can make wind chimes with these vertebrae. I'll give the glass float to Alma. I'll tell her how it reminded me of her braids. And Ty—Ty can scatter the bones of a bear among his apple trees.

Carrying the float, Joy climbed the basement stairs, comforted by the abrasive threads of netting around the glass ball. She would let all these things go. In the same way that she had somehow let go of their mother's and grandmother's habit of faith, while Alma had rediscovered hers. But it's my way to let it go. My love is like an open palm. If I set all these things down, now, this whole business of Grandma and Mom and their faith and their beliefs and their rituals, if I set all these down now and walk into my own life, if I don't come back here again, it doesn't mean I haven't been lavished with blessings.

The City Beneath the Snow

Mardy wore a corduroy hunting jacket of her father's, once bright orange, now faded to pink, loose enough to cover a bulky sweater. The knitted cuffs swallowed her hands; her fingers poked through like a child's. Her brother, Alan, was getting married this month, to his ex-wife. The accommodations they must have made to each other, to arrive at this turning, moved Mardy deeply—gave her a new wonder for the difficult secrets that people carried. Only the slowly freezing river, the sky barely holding back its burden of snow, seemed to return her mood.

The last scraps of faded birch leaves spiraled to the ground. The river gleamed like a mirror, holding the colors of woods and sky between its margins of ice. A wedding in this very house! Crepe ribbons to guide cars up the driveway. Guests would decorate the yard. Mardy picked up pieces of colored plastic from summer toys, the handle of a gun. The sky was heavy as milk.

Alan and Sonie had married the first time eighteen years ago at Sonie's church downtown. Sonie wore a dress with a high collar to cover the port wine stain that gripped the side of her neck. Seed pearls marched down from her collar over a substantial bosom to her small, tight waist. The impression of fierceness she always delivered contrasted with a sweet shape and satin-covered shoes. Sonie was smart as a whip and hardworking, but she didn't figure the world would ever return the favor. Normally she held her mouth firm and was not given to displays of emotion, to messages from her heart sent out willy-nilly with no expectation of return. Sonie measured every gesture, except for one thing: she liked to dance. She could spin for hours, she could waltz across Texas.

At their reception, a country music band had played all evening long. Mardy, only fourteen at that time, was transfixed; while her own family mostly stood around the food table, talking, Sonie and her relatives danced the two-step and "Cotton-Eyed Joe," hour after hour. Alan tried his best to keep up.

Sonie was twenty-two then. Now forty, she had changed. When she smiled now, her face was open, accessible. Not like before. Talking about Alan, she grinned, lavishly.

"We don't pay that much attention to each other," she told Mardy. "We don't concentrate so much on each other. It makes him wonderful to be with." She modeled her second wedding outfit, a soft dress of grayish blue wool, a tight waist, a wide, flaring skirt. It was the color of a wild bird. Sonie looked wonderful. But there was something she couldn't tell Mardy. Sonie's description of love was the skin of the orange. Whatever did make it work, and make it worthwhile, seemed locked in a different room of the house than any Mardy would ever enter.

Once, during their eight-year marriage, in a fit of resentment toward Alan, Sonie had gotten herself drunk, and Mardy had put her to bed. Washed her face, held her hand, and then reached down and kissed her cheek and temple. Her lips brushed Sonie's hair. She smoothed the hair back from the red stain on her neck. How soft and tender and sweet; so this is what men enjoy, Mardy thought with some surprise. Is this what I want?

In college Mardy had been distracted briefly, overwhelmingly, by a student in natural resources management. Her eyes leaped to follow the curve of his back as he bent to lace his Sorels. He impressed her with his confidence in the wilderness, his collection of trout flies. He lifted them out of their trays with square, heavy fingers and said, "Don't touch the hook." He wore a light brown Carhartt jacket stained with wood smoke. When they drew each other's blood in physiology class, the marble of his arm, the soft dark hair that lay on it like a suggestion, the veins that stood out and disappeared under his rolled-up sleeve terrified her. After eighteen years of nursing, she remembered that terror, and wondered at it.

Mardy certainly did not lead a sheltered life. At the ER she had taken in the victims and perpetrators of every violent act committed in this town. She was no longer surprised at what people did to each other, but she always turned to her patients with the detached though generous concern of someone passing through their lives. That part was easy.

There was a doctor, too, she sometimes thought about. Years ago, a neurosurgeon, a powerful man with thick shoulders, just beginning to build a solid paunch. They ate supper together at midnight in the hospital cafeteria. Sometimes she caught him looking at her with thoughtful black eyes. He would hold his violence back; she could tell, he would be incredibly gentle until the last minute—all that physical strength suggested self-control developed to a high degree, like his confidence that he could open a patient's brain with a microscopic edge. Until the last minute.

Then he left, to join another hospital. It was surgery he loved, not this place or anyone in it. She watched him say good-bye to another nurse, ball his fist and punch her gently in the shoulder. The playfulness of the gesture surprised Mardy. She went back to her desk and thought, *Did I read everything wrong?*

—

She stepped on another chunk of plastic—a purple gun that fired suction-tipped foam darts. The nephews, three of them, had finally worn down their parents' resistance to war toys. Uzis, bazookas, Roman swords had blossomed all summer long. Nephews and their friends died by the dozens on the lawn, their cheeks puffed out in constant sound effects. Warned not to leave anyone out, they'd go after the four-year-old. "Die, Molly," they'd say. "Come on, Molly. Die."

"I'm having my sister's ex-husband's brother perform the ceremony," Sonie had told her. "He's been made a marriage commissioner for the day. We're old friends. He's my something old. Worn and comfortable. Almost like the bridegroom," she added, and chuckled.

Old and worn and comfortable? Surely those were not the qualities that made Sonie hum and leave terribly thick brides' magazines sitting about and look at herself in the mirror so often, and think of nothing but one day?

And yet Alan and Sonie were coming back for seconds. Two lives together!

"Your sister's ex-husband's brother," Mardy repeated. "What do you call him?"

"Oh, now," said Sonie. "You'll like him. He has a way. Alan and I, we want to be—careless again."

"Careless?"

"Did I say that? I mean carefree. Really, Mardy, we have to cope with the embarrassment of having changed our minds already a number of times. In front of the same people. You call him Jim, that's his name. He's the accepting type. Since you haven't met him, I'm warning you."

"Against what?"

"Honey, he's cute."

"All right, I'm warned."

The day arrived, and with it the nephews, shy and awkward in their wedding finery. One wore a jacket of nubby linen; his slick hair sailed off the back of his head like the fin of a speedboat. His pockets bulged with toy soldiers. They had received differing advice from their parents on whether or not to tuck in their shirts, what color socks to wear.

Food and champagne were set out before the ceremony, and the children quickly discovered the bowl of chocolate sauce for the strawberries, and nearby a basket of sliced baguettes for a spinach dip. Ignoring berries and dip, they shoveled up the chocolate with the bread. It was a day to be left alone by the grownups, to circulate freely through the grownup world in that subterranean way children have. Amused by their own parents. They were the carefree ones, Mardy thought.

Her own heart seemed to have expanded, and if her paper cup with wedding bells printed on it had been made of glass, surely it would have shattered in her grip. There was too much happiness all around her; it was in the air; it was a general condition. Everyone bounced. Gravity had been repealed.

"He's here," Sonie sang out from the kitchen.

"All the world's a stage," said a strange, short, fat man, putting one foot up on the kitchen stool and clapping a hand over his heart. Mardy stared.

The ex-brother-in-law, the set-up, could he be this minor character? She was astonished at the disappointment that collided instantly in her chest with a rush of curiosity. He was her own height perhaps, definitely on the heavy side, with big hands—she noticed his hands right away—hands like clam shovels, one extended to her now. He had black hair and an intense, shy gaze, like a man treading water, hoping to break either forward or backward soon but at the instant supporting himself fairly well with his manners alone. He smiled. His teeth were very clean. A faint smell of some manly toiletry wafted her way. That was reassuring, as was his smile, genuinely kind. He knew they had been set up, too. Sonie has gone too far, Mardy thought. I am supposed to date this perfectly normal, decent looking, very short man?

"We're having a little champagne beforehand," she said, "as you can see. Would you like a cup?"

He looked at her paper wedding cup and at her.

"I wouldn't mind a cup of champagne."

"Jim, maybe we should practice," Sonie said, her white fingers suddenly appearing against the dark tweed of his arm. But she was looking across the room, her face blessed and unfocused in the steady current of manic joy. They made a nice couple, the two of them; when it came to size, they seemed made for each other. She dropped his arm and drifted away to someone else.

"What do you need to practice?" Mardy said.

He pulled out a paper from the inside pocket of his jacket—a gesture that always struck Mardy as exclusively and gracefully male—and unfolded it. "My lines," he said. "I want to get my lines right, for this solemn occasion."

"Oh, no."

"No?"

"We're drinking bubbles out of throwaway cups because this is a solemn occasion? Goodness, no. Weddings are, basically, silly. In a nice way, don't you think?"

He smiled instantly, not so much in agreement as in delight at her remark.

"Weightless events," he said. "Preposterous."

"Have you ever—are you..." she waved a hand at the room, not sure how to put her question.

"Oh, yes," he said. "Oh, yes, ancient history and lots of it. And yet, the heart snaps back. So, if not solemn, then worthwhile occasions."

"You must need to collect your thoughts right now. I should let you..."

"Collect my thoughts."

"Yes."

"Come here, you little devils."

"No, really."

"The badge of office is light," he said. "It was easy to obtain, and it'll be easy to take off. What do you suggest? Shall I stay a marriage commissioner the whole day, or just these ten minutes?"

"I'm sure I have no preference."

"I'm sure I have no preference," he repeated, smiling.

We're certainly getting off on a strange footing, Mardy thought. The sensation was not unpleasant.

"Shall we...?" called a voice, not Sonie's but the matron of honor's.

People immediately stiffened and clustered under doorframes. Sonie hiccupped softly into her bouquet and grinned at Alan. The matron of honor guided her into place and waved at the wedding guests. "Come," she said, and they stepped shyly into the living room, shuffled into a horseshoe and waited, quiet and obedient.

Jim, the short, heavy marriage commissioner, patted his tweed jacket and walked in front of the picture window. He stopped to watch a squirrel rob the birdfeeder, and then turned to face the solemn crowd. Mardy began to shake.

"Friends and family of Alan and Sonya," he began, looking at a piece of notebook paper. He paused and swung the paper down to his side. "What a lovely adventure this is, that we are so fortunate to witness. Few people travel down this road, the one made by two long and faithful memories. Few trust so much, to believe in their own, and their beloved's rebirth. For this is new to all of us.

"Alan and Sonya, who share a history, have surprised us with their new discovery of each other. Their willingness to say, 'I did not know you, after all.' They show us something new about devotion. They show us the strand of wonder, of amazement, usually so deeply buried in a relationship."

"We talk about certainty, but how little we know love, until we see brave and devoted and mature people turning to each other, with far less certainty than before. For they have known the unexpected, they have known disappointment. Look outside—there is no bounty forthcoming from nature. There is only what we make of ourselves, what we have in ourselves to offer. October. Now there's a month for love."

The paper he held against his thigh was fluttering. Mardy realized that his hand was shaking. She felt, herself, like a piece of soft and yielding yeasty dough that someone was impressing with his thumb and finger. Never in her life, or not in the past few years anyway, had she been so focused and still.

Jim pronounced them husband and wife. When Alan kissed Sonie, he picked her up off the ground; her light form disappeared in his arms, her blue-gray skirt swirled.

"I'd love you to see my new house," Jim said. She had just praised his wedding homily, but he was not poetic anymore. His fingertips shone with the grease of the fried mozzarella balls. As he rocked forward she realized that she was looking down at him. These new pumps were stupid shoes. It was unlike her to wear heels. She wanted to slide out of them.

"It's a throwback to the sixties," he went on. "It's got a conversation pit in the living room."

His lip, shaped like a bow, drew her eyes. She wanted to touch it with her finger. She ate something off her plate, not certain what it was—fruit, celery, a water chestnut?

Outside a few flakes of snow had begun to follow the last of the birch leaves through the milky afternoon, already coating the balloons tied all over the lawn.

"I mean what I say. You'd like my house. Or I'd like you to see it."

"Whoa," Mardy said. "I can't go."

"Why not?"

"I don't know you."

"Ah," he said. He touched her arm, his fingers on the loose silk of her blouse.

"That's true," he said. "That's very true. We don't know each other. Anything else?"

"No, nothing."

"Well, then. How easily we reach agreement. We find the salient things and we agree upon them. But I know myself, tonight I do, that is. And I know you are safe with me."

She had emptied her plate, without even looking down at it.

"It's snowing," he said. "It's too beautiful a night to be alone just yet."

She stood trembling on the edge. On the edge of a pier, watching a ship leave without her, again.

"It's snowing," he repeated. "Everything'll be different in the morning. Sneak out with me, now, Mardy, under cover of the snow."

"I'm scared."

He looked so touched, she stepped back in surprise. He held out his hand, his wide soft palm.

"Of me?" he said in amazement.

The conversation pit, a square, carpeted hole in the living room, made her laugh.

"I should remodel it, fill it in," he said. "It's a weird sort of thing. Forced casualness, isn't it?"

"Dated."

"The house is full of these touches," he said. And he took her hand, hooking his fingers into hers. Something happened inside her. They stood with their arms down, their fingers knitted together, and she closed her eyes, wanting it to last. Wanting the easiness to last.

"I've never done this," she said, suddenly. Sabotaging herself.

He said gently, unsurprised, "Never?"

"No."

"It doesn't matter." His free hand drifted to the front of her silk blouse. There was an expression of great tenderness on his face. "The feelings are in here, they all come from in here." He pressed his fingers gently against her waist. "In you, Mardy. Here is where they come from, and here is where they stay."

She took one step backward to haul in air.

"It's dark in here," she said.

"There's a light by the door," Jim said.

Her hand went out to the switch and paused. The switch plate was a naked man, grinning sheepishly. She stared at it in disbelief.

"What is this?"

"It was there when I moved in," Jim said. She looked at him, feeling reproach and shock, but the expression on his face held her: he looked chagrined.

It was only a switchplate. She flicked it and snorted. She looked back at Jim and wanted to rest her hands on his chest. There was a breast-bone and then a warm, firm, billow of flesh. Many nights of eating and drinking. A human being. Warm evidence of humanity. Her hands met his, and then went around him. Her heart pounded, but the flesh of his back, his head against hers, offered safety, concealment.

"Let's see what it's like over here," he said softly, drawing her toward the conversation pit. He piled pillows around her; she sensed the dark water outside, and her muscles stiffened until he lay on his side next to her and spoke into her hair.

"I won't tell you anything that isn't true," he said. "I will not do that. And you may tell me anything you like."

"Oh, my goodness," she said, putting her hand over his, where it lay on her stomach like a warm, sleeping animal.

All night long the snow fell, building a second city on top of the first. It was a city that for an instant only, the next morning, would lack all discriminating marks. For one instant only, before garage doors went up, before mittens were discovered to be lost, before feet became wet and cold, before people remembered all the things they had left outside that were now lost until spring—for that one moment the snow lay as it fell, weightless on the freezing river, the trees and fences and alleys, the low buildings of the city; so thick and fine and undisturbed it lay, you could not perceive the breathing of the dreamers within.

AFTERWORD

Marjorie Cole, who was my wife, was born in Boston in 1953. She studied at the University of Alaska and the University of Washington. She contributed in myriad ways to her community and was active in environmental, religious, arts, political, and literary efforts both in Alaska and nationally. Among other things, she walked across Spain, founded Call to Action Alaska, gardened, played the banjo, read at every chance she got, and took immoderate pride in her sons Henry and Desmond Cole.

Marjorie was a prodigious writer. Her stories and poems, as well as essays on travel, writing, religion, and the environment, appeared in dozens of noted literary journals, magazines, and newspapers. She published well over a hundred book reviews, contributed chapters to anthologies, was a frequent participant in writers' conferences, and was the author of three earlier books. Her first novel, *Correcting the Landscape*, was winner of the prestigious Bellwether Prize for Fiction. She lived in Ester, Alaska, and died in December 2009 from cholangiocarcinoma, a cancer.

I would like to thank the University of Alaska Press for taking on this project, with special thanks to the following people associated in one way or another with the press: Wanda Chin, Dixon Jones, Taya Kitaysky, Sue Mitchell, Peggy Shumaker, Amy Simpson, and Joeth Zucco. Several writer friends of Marjorie's provided invaluable criticism and encouragement as the stories were being written and their contribution is warmly acknowledged. Particularly I am grateful to Jean Anderson, for impressing on me the value of this endeavor, for helping to select the stories that comprise the collection, for carefully reading the manuscript, for excellent suggestions, and for her generosity, enthusiasm, and friendship.

Marjorie had plans for other writing, and she had plans for other walks:

Someday, I announce, I'm going to keep walking
for a thousand miles, two thousand.
Won't carry a backpack.
Just for the thrill of it, fling out my legs
across this landscape. Why should I stop?
You come, too.

—from her poem, "Rattlesnake Country"

Pat Lambert
September 2011